○ ○ ○ ○ ○ ○ ○ ○ ■ ◆ ○ ○ ○ ■ ◆ ◇ ◆ ♦ ○ ■ ◆ ◇ ■ ◇ ○ ○ ○ ■ ○

THE RELATIONSHIP
PROBLEM SOLVER
FOR LOVE, MARRIAGE,
AND DATING

■ ■ ◇ ○ ◇ ■ ■

○ ○ ○ ○ ○ ○ ■ ◆ ○ ○ ○ ■ ◆ ◇ ◆ ♦ ○ ■ ◆ ◇ ■ ◇ ○ ○ ○ ■ ○ ○

ALSO BY KELLY E. JOHNSON, M.D.

A Relationship for a Lifetime:
Everything You Need to Know to Create a Love That Lasts

♦ ♦ ♦

OTHER HAY HOUSE TITLES OF RELATED INTEREST

Books

Feng Shui Dos & Taboos for Love, by Angi Ma Wong

Getting Unstuck: 8 Simple Steps to Solving Any Problem,
by Dr. Joy Browne

How to Ruin Your Love Life, by Ben Stein
(available August 2003)

The Mystery and Magic of Love: Once the Mind
is Infused with Love, Only Eternal Joy is Experienced,
by Krishan Chopra, M.D.

Pathways to the Soul: 101 Ways to Open Your Heart,
by Carlos Warter, M.D., Ph.D.

Secrets of Attraction: The Universal Laws of Love, Sex,
and Romance, by Sandra Anne Taylor

Card Decks

Heart and Soul (a 50-card deck), by Sylvia Browne

I Can Do It® Cards: Affirmations for Romance,
by Louise L. Hay

Manifesting Good Luck Cards: Love and Relationships,
by Deepak Chopra (available August 2003)

MarsVenus Cards, by John Gray

All of the above are available at your local bookstore,
or may be ordered through Hay House, Inc.:

(800) 654-5126 or **(760) 431-7695**
(800) 650-5115 (fax) or **(760) 431-6948 (fax)**
www.hayhouse.com

THE RELATIONSHIP PROBLEM SOLVER FOR LOVE, MARRIAGE, AND DATING

Kelly E. Johnson, M.D.

Hay House, Inc.
Carlsbad, California • Sydney, Australia
Canada • Hong Kong • United Kingdom

Published and distributed in the United States by: Hay House, Inc.,
P.O. Box 5100, Carlsbad, CA 92018-5100 • *Phone:* (760) 431-7695 or (800)
654-5126 • *Fax:* (760) 431-6948 or (800) 650-5115 • www.hayhouse.com •
Published and distributed in Australia by: Hay House Australia Pty Ltd,
18/36 Ralph St., Alexandria NSW 2015 • *Phone:* 612-9669-4299 • *Fax:* 612-
9669-4144 • *e-mail:* info@hayhouse.com.au • **Published and Distributed
in the United Kingdom by:** Hay House UK, Ltd. • Unit 202, Canalot Stu-
dios • 222 Kensal Rd., London W10 5BN • *Phone:* 020-8962-1230 • *Fax:*
020-8962-1239 • **Distributed in Canada by:** Raincoast • 9050 Shaugh-
nessy St., Vancouver, B.C. V6P 6E5 • *Phone:* (604) 323-7100 • *Fax:* (604)
323-2600

Design: Summer McStravick

Library of Congress Cataloging-in-Publication Data

Johnson, Kelly E.
 The relationship problem solver for love, marriage, and dating / Kelly E.
Johnson.
   p. cm.
 ISBN 1-40190-126-3 (pbk.)
 1. Man-woman relationships. 2. Interpersonal conflict. 3. Dating (Social
customs) 4. Marriage. I. Title.
 HQ801 .J5934 2003
 306.7—dc21

                        2002152322

ISBN 1-4019-0126-3

06 05 04 03   4 3 2 1
1st printing, May 2003

Printed in the United States of America

○ ○ ○ ○ ○ ○ ○ ○ ■ ◇ ○ ○ ○ ■ ◇ ◇ ◆ ◆ ○ ■ ◇ ◇ ■ ◇ ○ ○

This book is dedicated to my wife, Betsy,
whom I love deeply

To my parents,
who both set a great example of how
to make a relationship succeed

And to anyone who desires to have a
love relationship that lasts a lifetime

■ ■ ◇ ○ ◇ ■ ■

○ ○ ○ ○ ■ ◇ ○ ○ ○ ■ ◇ ◇ ◆ ◆ ○ ■ ◇ ◇ ■ ◇ ○ ○ ○ ■ ○ ○

CONTENTS

♦ ♦ ♦

Please note: All of the stories and
case studies in this book are true. All names have
been changed for confidentiality purposes.

(**Editor's note:** For you grammar purists out there, we at
Hay House realize that the use of *their, they,* and *them* to refer
to singular individuals throughout this book is grammatically
incorrect. However, we want to avoid awkward "he/she"
"him/her" constructions. Thank you for your understanding!)

ACKNOWLEDGMENTS

The book you now hold is obviously the product of many people—much time and effort has been spent to ensure that my writing is of the highest quality possible. I certainly owe a debt of gratitude to all of the following people who have stood by me and put up with all of my little quirks and idiosyncrasies.

I thank my wife, Betsy, for her undying optimism. When I'm having a bad day, she's always there to listen to me and support me, and she's taught me a lot about the virtues of patience and tolerance. She is truly my partner for life.

To my friends and family: I still feel the same about all of you now as I did when I wrote my first book. I'm extremely lucky to have such great people in my life . . . and you've all taught me something about problem solving by your examples.

To the staff at Hay House: a huge thank-you. You believed in me enough to publish this second book and have all been wonderful. A special nod goes to the publicity staff—Jacqui Clark, Chandra Teitscheid, and Tonya Toone—who helped "spread the word" and tolerated my weird sense of humor. Also, I offer heartfelt appreciation to my editors, Jill Kramer and Shannon Littrell. My manuscript was certainly in good hands.

Finally, to you, the reader, I give thanks that you have once again let me into your life for a brief time. I sincerely wish you much success and happiness in your love relationships.

INTRODUCTION

W hen I'm in the market for a new book, I usually ask myself the following question: *What is it going to do for me?* I then size up what a particular volume has to offer and either buy it or put it back on the shelf. This is especially true with self-help and relationship books, because the choices are so numerous. I've personally read countless works over the years that promise to deliver the keys to relationship success but then become overly theoretical and dense, or talk about vague concepts that sound good on paper but are impossible to apply effectively each day.

The Relationship Problem Solver for Love, Marriage, and Dating is different. First of all, I'm going to tell you what you're getting right up front—that way, there won't be any surprises or disappointments halfway through your reading experience.

I'm sure I'm not the first one to ever tell you this, but your relationship is going to have problems at some point! Be they small quibbles or virtual life-destroyers, I can just about guarantee that *something* will inevitably arise, and you'll wish that you had a reference guide to address the problem and offer practical guidance and solutions. Well, have no fear—this book *is* that guide. I hope it will become an invaluable resource for years to come.

In my first book, *A Relationship for a Lifetime,* I challenged readers to view their lives and love relationships in an entirely different way. Many people took this challenge, and the response I got was overwhelmingly positive (to say the least!). These readers did the work and got their act together—as a result, their relationships are more honest, happy, and real.

You see, there's simply no substitute for a little knowledge to help when you and your partner reach a critical juncture in your lives. Without some basic knowledge of several core relationship principles, you'll always have to fly by the seat of your pants, never having a safety net when the going gets rough.

Will we stay together? Are we even right for each other? Do we want the same things out of life? Is there a way to put some passion back into our relationship? These are the questions that many of us have faced at one point or another in our relationships. But more important is this concern: *Why can't we just get along?*

This simply stated, yet incredibly complex, question is the basis for this book.

Your Problems <u>Can</u> Be Solved!

Over the years, I've been told many times that women are generally the ones who want to learn about relationships and are more interested in the mechanics of communication and intimacy than men. Maybe there's some truth to the notion that guys just want to be left alone to do their own thing, hoping that problems will magically go away as they continue to engage in the very behavior that caused the problem in the first place.

Sure, this may be true for some males, but it's been my experience that most men actually do want a conflict-free relationship as much as women do—it's just not natural for them to intuitively sense how to easily solve these types of problems. Until now, there hasn't been a simple and straight-forward road map for men to follow, so they've given up, secretly wishing that their wives would just stop nagging.

With that in mind, I decided to write a comprehensive manual on relationship-conflict management that's easy to read and practical to apply on an everyday basis. If you're a woman, you may want to suggest to your man that this book is a step-by-step set of instructions that can elim-inate arguments related to a wide variety of topics. (After all, everyone likes less arguing and tension.) If you're a man, then I've done you a big favor by breaking down com-plicated points of disagreement into digestible bites. This isn't complicated stuff once some basic negotiating tac-tics are learned. I won't bore you with a lot of theory—you'll get "just the facts, ma'am." And it will certainly be time well spent, because you'll learn how to avoid and ease relationship pain.

Since you and your partner have most likely never taken a course on the basics of relationship problem solving, think of this book as that course. So now when a serious disagree-ment about money, sex, careers, family, or household chores arises, you'll have something at your fingertips that pro-vides you with some immediate and practical guidance. Solutions can only arise from open communication that is practical and pertinent. Life is short, so it makes no sense to waste your time being mad at each other when there's so much joy to experience once you're both on the same page.

Managing Conflicts

One of the most critical ideas I expressed in my first book was actually in the final chapter. I put forth the concept of *the relationship pyramid,* which is illustrated below. Take the time to really study what the pyramid consists of. You'll notice that at its base is the challenge of

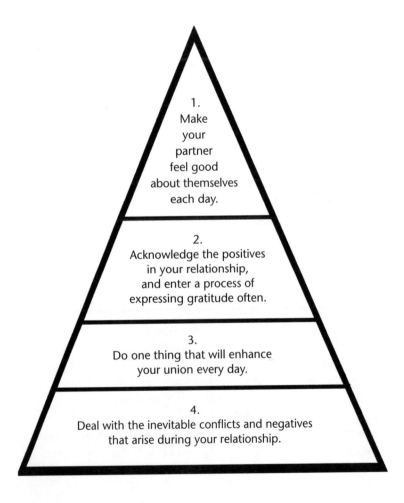

1.
Make
your
partner
feel good
about themselves
each day.

2.
Acknowledge the positives
in your relationship,
and enter a process of
expressing gratitude often.

3.
Do one thing that will enhance
your union every day.

4.
Deal with the inevitable conflicts and negatives
that arise during your relationship.

managing the inevitable conflicts that arise during the course of the relationship. Since this is sadly the spot where most of us spend a lot of our time and energy dealing with our partners, I decided to focus on the base of that pyramid in this book.

Most of us find that a problem pops up, we try to dispose of it, and then we don't give it another thought until the next time it rears its ugly head. The flaw with this approach, however, is that the problem never gets dealt with in a way that puts it to rest for good. We're then trapped in a cycle of arguments that lessens our ability to experience loving feelings. Before we know what's happened, we feel only negativity and bitterness toward our mates.

The overall goal, then, is for us to alter the course of relationship differences so that we're free to live in a loving environment, instead of one characterized by anger and rage. You may not think that this is possible, because your relationships may have always been filled with disappointments and frustrations. Your relationship equation might currently look like this:

Relationship problem + negative, emotionally based response = failure

There's a new approach, however, which will be outlined in the rest of this book, and which gives your relationship a chance at achieving the following outcome:

Relationship problem + positive, proactive, and objective response = success!

Note that the probability of success depends upon an *objective* analysis of the situation. When you don't prepare for a relationship discussion, only emotional reactions will result, and they usually get out of hand. Hurt feelings lead to lashing out—in other words, a new problem arises out of the failed attempt to solve the original problem! Luckily, though, things can be different if you and your partner are willing to do a little preventive work to thwart problems before they begin. Reason will then take the place of anger, and you'll both ultimately get what's best for the relationship.

Charting the Course of True Love

William Shakespeare offered up a great and timeless quote in his play *A Midsummer's Night Dream:* "The course of true love never did run smooth." I don't know what kind of love affairs *he* had in his life, but he was certainly on to something there. Although love is sometimes a stormy and turbulent experience, it can be transformed into a smooth, pleasant ride. All it takes is two people who are both willing to negotiate *before* the arguments begin.

Your learning process starts here. Keep in mind that relationships end not because of differences of opinion in many crucial areas, but because two partners don't have any system for solving their problems effectively. With that said, let's move on to the way I've laid out this book.

Part I will cover a general discussion of the hows and whys of relationship conflicts. This will give us a framework upon which to build specific solutions to specific problems. Part II will focus on a specific hotspot that can cause much grief in your relationship. The titles of the chapters are pretty self-explanatory, so you can quickly get to the pertinent information if things around you are falling apart or you just "can't take it anymore." For example, the chapter on money will designate the five main areas that must be negotiated and navigated through to be able to defuse huge conflicts later on.

In each chapter, I offer specific points for you to ponder. I cannot state strongly enough how vital it is for you to address these first by yourself and then with your partner. It's important to know the way you each feel, but the idea is to work together to find what works and feels comfortable for *your* relationship—your specific answers may be entirely different from that of your friends or other couples you know. (Even if you're currently single, this is required reading so that you have a relationship solution before a conflict ever occurs.)

So how do you go about broaching some awkward discussions with your partner? I know it isn't easy to say, "Let's talk about our sex life," or "Your spending habits just don't work for our relationship," or "You do some things that really annoy me!" so why not say that you just read this book, which has some interesting ideas, and ask your partner to check them out. Then start with your most problematic area, roll up your sleeves, and sit down at the dinner table and hammer out some solutions that work for both of you. Even if, for instance, your relationship is doing all right in the area of communication, at some point there may be trouble ahead. I liken this to doing the preventive maintenance checks on all of your car's parts before a breakdown occurs.

Don't allow your relationship to get to the point of no return. The arguing *can* stop; there *are* answers to your problems. You now have a great place to start. You can be the captain who navigates your own relationship. With just a little effort, your relationship can truly reach its full potential—a loving, intimate bond that's based on fairness and respect.

Let's get started.

PART I

WHY ARE YOU FIGHTING?

CHAPTER 1

THE NATURE OF RELATIONSHIP CONFLICT

W hy do you fight with the person you love? I never used to understand how two people could fall madly in love, pledge their lives to each other, and then spend the rest of their time tearing the relationship apart. One day I was talking separately to a couple of friends when the truth finally hit me. You see, their relationship was on the rocks, and both of them had recruited me to save the day, albeit on the sly. I spent several hours talking to the wife and became convinced that her husband was the problem; then I spent some time with the husband and was sure that his *wife* was in the wrong. As a psychiatrist, I pride myself on objectivity and the ability to see all sides of a given situation, but I was really confused here.

Then I figured it out: I was trying to identify the "bad guy." Each person in this couple saw the other as the villain, but the truth was that they were both individually very bright, wonderful people. They both had great careers, lots of friends, and supportive families. Their wedding was beautiful, and it seemed that the sky was the limit. They'd purchased a beautiful home, and on the surface, seemed to settle comfortably into their new life together. There really was no bad guy, yet the relationship crashed and burned. The problem was that this couple just couldn't overcome their personal differences.

The moral of this story is a powerful lesson in relationship dynamics. This is something that you should remember throughout the rest of the book as we look at specific relationship problems that can get in your way.

I've noticed three particular things as I've counseled couples, and they're what I call "Conflict Points." Here's **Conflict Point #1**:

○ ○ ■ ◇ ◇　　◆ ◆ ○ ■ ○

An intimate relationship is an extremely stressful experience that can bring out the worst traits in two otherwise reasonable people.

○ ○ ■ ◇ ◇　　◆ ◆ ○ ■ ○

Most people who end up in failed relationships are, for the most part, decent and kind—but you wouldn't be able to tell it by the crazy and off-the-wall behavior both sides exhibit when the relationship hits the skids. I've had couples in my office screaming so loudly at each other that everyone down the hall could hear their entire exchange. A guy who had the office next to mine would occasionally pop his head in and ask, "You okay?" before realizing it was just another couples-therapy session.

After many years of seeing relationships with fantastic potential come to an end, I finally put it all together:

Great people can have horrible relationships because they can't handle their differences of opinion and conflicting needs. And remember this other little caveat of human behavior—success at work or with friends has virtually nothing to do with success in an intimate, loving, monogamous relationship. The reason is simple, as stated in **Conflict Point #2**:

○ ○ ■ ◇ ◇ ◆ ◆ ○ ■ ○

All of our unresolved issues from childhood and other difficult relationships will be magnified tenfold in the context of intimacy.

○ ○ ■ ◇ ◇ ◆ ◆ ○ ■ ○

It's relatively easy to keep things nice and light in the boundaries of work and friendly acquaintances, but it's nearly impossible to do this within the confines of love and commitment because the stakes are much higher. Deep emotional feelings can lead to a lifetime of happiness, but they can also breed insecurity, fear, and resentment over time. Visually, think of it this way: You unpack your emotional baggage, your partner unpacks their emotional baggage, you mix it all up . . . and that's a lot of bags to sort through and carry around.

Realize that your partner is going to push your buttons sometimes. What this means in practical terms is that it really doesn't matter how nice you both are individually—what counts is whether you can sort out problems and still be nice *to each other*. This leads us to **Conflict Point #3**:

○ ○ ■ ◇ ◇   ◆ ◆ ○ ■ ○

Like it or not, you and your partner will have different views and opinions on important relationship topics. If you can't tolerate and embrace these differences, then you should have stayed by yourself. Negotiating around these differences is the real challenge of the relationship.

○ ○ ■ ◇ ◇   ◆ ◆ ○ ■ ○

A System to Finally Stop the Fighting

I've been asked just about every permutation of relationship question over the course of my career, but the one I'm asked most frequently is the following: "How do we stop fighting?" You name the type of disagreement, and I'm sure I've heard about it over the years. That's why I've devoted entire chapters of this book to the main topics that people fight about.

However, if you think about it in a general sense, there are only a few basic different reasons why we don't always get along (outlined in the next chapter). This is extremely important, because if you and your partner are able to understand the basic root cause of any particular conflict, then you will have completed the first step in solving the problem. So let's look at a general system to deal with relationship conflict.

Step 1: Make an ironclad agreement with your partner to stop yelling at and berating each other; instead, agree to use a basic system to solve your differences every single time. You can stop the fighting if you make a pact to talk in calm, restrained voices. Don't tell me that this is impossible, because anyone has the capability to hold their temper if they put their mind to it. The next time voices get raised, just think, *We're getting nowhere fast. This* *won't solve our differences; it will only make things worse.* I can assure you that repeated episodes of verbal abuse and arguments with no end in sight will destroy your relationship, or at a minimum, make each of you incredibly unhappy. If you *both* aren't willing to do this basic step right at the beginning, then the rest of the steps are really meaningless. You may as well put this book down right now.

If you'd like to continue, then in the next day—that's right, within 24 hours—I want you to meet with your partner and agree that all yelling and screaming will stop, if for no other reason than that it's the respectful thing to do. Sit right across from each other and say these words: "I will try at all times to be nice to you and do whatever I can to avoid an angry outburst." If you say it out loud, it will have more power as a promise to be upheld! I know of many couples who always talk things out in a reasonable manner—you can adopt this way of interacting, too.

Step 1 is the foundation on which everything else is built. **Step 2** (identifying reasons), **step 3** (negotiating) and **step 4** (resolution) will be described in detail in Chapters 2, 3, and 4, respectively. The issue you disagree upon simply doesn't matter—it could be something as small as who washes the dishes after dinner, or as big a decision as where you'll live or how many children you'll have. The process should always be the same:

> **Step 1:** Agree not to get angry and not to yell at each other (Chapter 1).
>
> **Step 2:** Identify the real reason why you or your partner is angry (Chapter 2).
>
> **Step 3:** Negotiate and compromise in a cooperative spirit (Chapter 3).
>
> **Step 4:** End the disagreement and resolve the issue (Chapter 4).

Before you read any further, take a second and memorize these steps.

Now let's go on to the second step and identify the four main reasons *why* you and your partner have conflicts that could threaten the very fabric of your loving relationship. Keep them in mind as you read the rest of the book.

CHAPTER 2

THE REAL REASONS WHY YOU CAN'T GET ALONG

At some point during the course of any intimate relationship, you're going to get mad. You're going to be so angry at the person you love that smoke comes out of your ears. Believe me, if you're capable of intense loving feelings toward your partner, then you're quite able to feel intense anger and rage for them, too. When you love someone, things matter much more, and your feelings can be hurt on a deeper level. This doesn't mean that you're an emotional wreck—it simply means that you're human, with unchecked human emotions.

With that said, let's identify the four main reasons why you fight. This is **Step 2** in your quest for conflict resolution.

◆ ◆ ◆

Argument #1: You Don't Give Me What I Want!

I'm going to assume that you're not a childish brat who can never be satisfied no matter how hard your partner tries; nor are you a doormat who's afraid to ask for anything. Chances are, you're probably somewhere in between, which means that you have certain reasonable needs that you'd like your partner to fulfill.

There's absolutely nothing wrong with asking for what you want. It isn't selfish, and it certainly doesn't mean you're a bad person. You deserve to have a partner who at least tries to satisfy you, even if it takes some effort and compromise. Problems spring from unmet expectations. It may be helpful to look at the origin of these expectations, but that still won't change the fact that if you expect your partner to act in a certain way, you'll become quite angry when they fail to do so. The chain of events is simple to diagram:

You expect something from your partner—►they don't come through for you—►you get angry.

I know that this seems like a very basic concept that everyone should understand, but believe me, most people can't even identify their own initial need, which starts the whole chain reaction. They just know that they aren't getting "something," so they end up feeling cheated or constantly disappointed by their partner. This in itself is enough to cause major conflicts and intensely angry moments. Of course, it works in reverse, too—sometimes *you* may not give your partner what *they* need.

Why do you feel angry when you don't get what you want? Wouldn't it make more sense to sit down and calmly tell your partner how frustrated you are? Of course it would, but that's not how human beings act at times. It's as if you have an internal switch that gets flipped, causing you to react in the only way you can: yelling in anger. Unfortunately, by this point there's little likelihood that you're going to get what you want, since your partner will only hear the tone, and not the content, of your demand. This can be further shown in the next sequence in our angry chain reaction:

> You get angry——➤ your partner reacts defensively and can't hear the content——➤ an argument ensues——➤ you have virtually no chance of getting what you want.

Finally, when your expectation goes unmet once more, you get upset again . . . and the whole cycle repeats itself over and over. Many couples spend their entire relationship in this cycle, which usually results in the end of that union.

Can this scenario be avoided? The answer is a resounding *yes*, but first we must do a little work. Now if you're like a lot of people in relationships, you just expect things to be magically done for you without telling your partner exactly what you want. Well, I didn't marry a psychic, and in all likelihood, neither did you. What I mean is that your partner can't read your mind and automatically cater to all of your whims! I wrote about this concept in my first book, *A Relationship for a Lifetime*, but it's so important that it bears repeating: *If you're not able to get exactly what you want in your relationship, then it's ultimately your fault!* You can protest this all you want, but it's a fact. If you need something specific, then it's up to you to ask for it!

I once counseled a woman who was frequently angry with her husband because he didn't clean up the garage when he'd finished working in there. She admitted to me that she'd never actually told him her expectation—so how was he to know that she was offended?

There is a way to avoid this type of situation: *Define what you want from your partner, and then communicate it.* Your expectation may still go unmet, but at least you'll have given it a shot. (We'll talk about what to do if your partner refuses to change in a later chapter.)

At this point in the process, I'd like you to do the following, which I call the "How to get what I need" approach. This may be the most critical exercise that I ask you to do, so don't blow it off. You and your partner should both do the exercise and then share the results with each other.

Fill in the blanks of the following sentence:

I'd like my partner to _____, and I expect _____ and _____.

This can obviously cover a wide variety of subjects, and if there are hundreds of things you can think of, then you may need to write this sentence hundreds of times. I know that it may feel like I've asked you to stay after school and finish your homework, but this isn't punishment—it's a crucial step in getting what you want and deserve.

To make this exercise easier, I'll give you a tip on how to get started. Look at the chapter topics I've selected for this book (such as money, sex, family, and so forth) and systematically identify what you want in each of these areas. At this point, no expectation is too crazy to write down—you'll find out soon enough if your partner thinks that your needs are completely over the top!

For example, if you require sex three times a week, write it down. If you'd like to engage in a conversation every evening, then write it down. If you want to go out to dinner every Saturday night, write it down. If you'd prefer that your mate stop watching TV all the time and pay attention to you, write it down. I knew someone who expected her husband to give her a foot massage each night, and she told him so. I'm not sure if this would be my cup of tea, but her husband was fine with her request. The bottom line was that she defined what she wanted, verbalized it, and got it. She had no further reason to be angry, so at least that part of their relationship flourished.

To sum up: Lessen your anger regarding unmet expectations by first defining the need and then asking for it. You may be pleasantly surprised when your partner fulfills your desire, but nothing great is ever going to happen unless you take a chance and *ask*.

Argument #2: You Don't Listen to Me!

Many researchers over the years have asked women to state their biggest complaint about men. It probably won't surprise you to learn that one of the most popular has been: "He never hears what I say." Even I, a professional who gets paid to listen to people, am often accused of "selective hearing" by my wife. I have to admit that sometimes I hear what she says, but it just doesn't register until I've been told for the third time. But trust me, she persists until I know what she needs. That's all right with me—it's our little rhythm and we both know it.

It's certainly not fun to be ignored by your partner, especially when it's something that you really feel strongly about. This reminds me of a woman I once treated named Linda. She complained to me for months that her husband, Jim, never responded to any of her requests. Linda claimed that his behavior often made her quite angry, and when she'd yell at him, he'd accuse her of being mean-spirited and rude. I found it hard to believe that he *never* tried to respond to her wishes, so I suggested that she bring him in to one of our sessions.

What I noticed very quickly was that Linda was right— even in an environment where it was acceptable to say *anything,* Jim said nothing. I'd ask him to rephrase what Linda had just expressed, and most of the time he had no idea and acted as if he could have cared less. It was not only infuriating to Linda, but to me as well. I correctly predicted that their marriage would collapse because Jim showed zero respect for his wife's needs. He didn't care to listen if it involved any amount of work on his part.

This, of course, is an extreme case, but there are varying degrees of not being heard—and it all puts a huge strain on the relationship. For instance, I'm sure that you've had the experience of your partner looking you right in the eye, acknowledging what you said, and then proceeding to engage in the exact opposite behavior. It's as if you said: "Please pick your clothes up off the floor," and they heard: "Please throw all of your clothes on the floor so I can pick them up." That's enough to unhinge anyone.

I ultimately can't tell you why your partner won't listen to your needs. There are any number of reasons why this happens: Perhaps you're involved with a passive-aggressive person, and on some level they like to upset you; maybe your partner never likes to be told "what to do"; or it's possible that the person you love couldn't care less about developing communication skills and does their own thing at your expense. Whatever the reason, the outcome is certain: When you feel ignored, your feelings get hurt and you're more likely to lash out with anger. Your partner's attempt to avoid a conflict (by not responding) causes another argument in itself.

It's key to tell your partner that their habit of not listening will only lead to increased relationship tension between the two of you. It's one thing to disagree on a particular issue if both people are at least talking, but it's quite another to feel as if you're talking to a brick wall.

So how can you increase the odds that your complaints will actually be taken seriously? Remember this next concept and your luck may change: *It's all in the presentation.* You've got to deliver your message properly or the content will just get lost in the shuffle.

To that end, I'm now going to present some communication techniques that should really work—so your partner will actually stop watching TV long enough to hear what you say.

The Straightforward Approach

Tell your partner: "Look, this issue is really important to me, so I'd just like a few moments to discuss it with you. I promise not to yell at you—I just want to talk."

Hopefully, this will grab them long enough so that you can tell them what you need. However, it may not, so let's go on to the next tactic, which is a little more forceful.

The Feelings Approach

Say: "When you walk away or ignore me, it really hurts my feelings. Even if you don't agree with me, I wish that you'd at least respect my right to express myself."

If you're still not heard, then you have a choice to make. If the issue doesn't warrant immediate attention, you may want to try again later and hope for the best. If it has to be examined right now, then you'd better pull out your full ammunition and demand to be heard.

The Demanding Approach

Assertively state: "You can choose to walk away, but this issue is going to have to be dealt with at some point in the very near future. If you won't at least try to hear me, then your actions could have serious long-term consequences for our relationship."

If this doesn't open any lines of communication, you have much bigger problems to solve—namely, that you have a rude partner who just doesn't care about your happiness.

♦ ♦ ♦

Notice that none of the above approaches involves yelling or screaming, which simply won't work if you truly want to be heard. You must get your partner to focus on the content of your request rather than causing them to react defensively to your angry tone. Think of these techniques as a little lesson in Communication 101 and you should see some positive results. You certainly deserve a partner who will at least make an attempt to consider your feelings, because it shows basic respect and indicates a willingness to work together. If this isn't the case, you'll probably need to deal with the next point.

Argument #3: You Don't Do Anything!

Actually, this encompasses two arguments: "You don't do anything I ask you to do!" and "You do whatever you want without asking me if it's okay!" If I put a tape recorder in a room when you and your partner argue, I bet I'd hear some form of those statements shouted out. It's that common.

It's infuriating to ask someone for help and get nothing but an empty promise in return. How many times have you heard, "I'll get to it," and then your partner never does get to it? You both go around in a cycle of demanding and promising—you demand, your partner promises, they break the promise, and you have to demand again—until you really blow your stack or give up and do it yourself.

And don't think that your partner doesn't know exactly what they're doing. I once had an acquaintance who would "forget" to clean up the house because he knew that after his wife finished complaining, she'd do the chores herself. He didn't care what she said since her threats were meaningless. As he proudly told me, "It goes in one ear and out the other!" Of course, this was just what his mother used to do—yell and then clean up all his messes, while he tuned her out and never had to suffer any consequences. This guy got a new mother in his wife, and his wife (unfortunately) married a child.

Take a moment to think of the infinite number of situations that fall into this category. Here are just a few:

- Your partner never makes you feel special—that is, they forget anniversaries and birthdays, they don't compliment you on your appearance or accomplishments, they don't ever surprise you with the occasional gift or card, and so on.

- You have to do the majority of the undesirable work in the relationship, such as cleaning the house, paying the bills, taking care of the kids, doing the cooking, running the errands . . . while your partner refuses to help or makes lots of excuses.

- After you ask your partner to perform a specific action, it doesn't get done on a timely basis, if at all.

- Your partner has an agenda and schedule that has nothing to do with you; there's no spirit of teamwork. This category includes a partner who goes out with friends whether you like it or not, a partner who spends money without consulting you, or one who makes plans for leisure activities without your input.

- Your partner is just plain lazy and tries to force you to make all of the major decisions. You're put in the position of keeping the relationship going, while your partner is just "along for the ride."

If any of these scenarios sound familiar, then you're with someone who's only interested in their own comfort level. This dynamic won't work for the relationship in the long run, because you'll become resentful and see your partner as a self-centered jerk.

So if the arguments you tend to have with your significant other fall into this general category, what should you do?

First, you must make a commitment to yourself that you won't let them get away with it any longer! This means that you'll demand that your partner contribute an equal amount of time and work to the relationship and work *with* you, not *against* you. Notice I said *demand*, not *ask*—once in a while you have the right to demand certain actions. Make sure that you stick to your guns, though. Laziness breeds more laziness, and your partner has to know what's required for your happiness.

Second, tell yourself that it's okay to want some romance and quality time from your partner. And you shouldn't feel guilty for wanting someone to pull their own weight—you weren't put on this planet to be your partner's maid, cook, and butler. If you're really getting the respect you deserve, then there should be a spirit of generosity and helpfulness in your relationship.

Third, sit down and divide up the unpleasant duties. I often suggest that couples write down the actual tasks to be completed so there's absolutely no question as to who did or didn't do their fair share. Make up a schedule, for that will ensure success. I know that nobody wants to be the one to clean the bathroom, but *someone* has to do it, and it shouldn't be you every time.

Fourth, demand that major decisions be made jointly. I'm acquainted with someone who went out and bought a house in a different city without consulting his wife first! I know it sounds incredible, but it's true. I found it even harder to believe that this man's wife ultimately went along with the plan. The two subsequently split up, and now they're living in different cities.

I'll talk in detail about money management in a later chapter, but suffice it to say that you don't want to get into debt and have your credit rating ruined because your partner spent a lot of money behind your back—major decisions such as these should be made as a team.

Finally, remember that the longer you let a lazy partner get away with this type of behavior, the harder it will be for any change to occur. So make your demands today.

Argument #4: You Hurt My Feelings!

It's a given that you're occasionally going to get your feelings hurt in a relationship. After all, if you plan on relating to other people on any kind of intimate level, then there will be times when they say something that really digs deep. Hopefully these words will be said unintentionally, and you'll make up and go on. Your significant other should never deliberately say mean things to you or consistently be inconsiderate. I can't tell you the number of people I've seen who get treated with disrespect in their intimate relationship, but then say it's all right because "We love each other." This is just unacceptable—the outcome can only be a lowering of self-esteem.

Here's a little exercise I'd like you and your partner to try in the next day or so. I'll bet that both of you will be quite surprised by the results, and you may even start to treat each other with more consideration.

For one week I want you each to keep track of every remark or action emanating from your partner that you consider disrespectful or hurtful. Don't overanalyze your reactions too much or worry about whether you're justified or not. Then, at the end of the week (and not before!), share your lists with each other.

The point of this exercise isn't to dwell on a laundry list of complaints, but to open up a line of communication. A lot of times your partner may not even know the things that make you feel bad about yourself. So this isn't just an educational experience—it's also a way to initiate a process of respect and kindness toward one another. I know that you can pull this off because I've seen many other couples benefit greatly from it.

The key is to say out loud that your feelings were hurt, and to then tell your partner why their actions or words seemed so disrespectful. For example, if remarks were made about your weight, the process would go something like this:

"On Wednesday you called me fat and said that I should lose some weight before we can have good sex again. That really hurt my feelings and made me feel bad about myself."

I know this may be difficult for you to say, but the alternative is to allow a pattern of spiteful remarks to continue. It seems only fair to let your partner know what bothers you so they have a chance to change.

At this point you may be thinking of worst-case scenarios, such as your partner not taking this seriously at all and continuing to be mean-spirited or rude to you. Maybe you're envisioning your partner trying to talk you out of your emotions with statements such as: "That shouldn't hurt your feelings," or "What's the big deal? Get over it and stop acting like a baby!" In either case, if you do get this type of response, you've got larger problems in the relationship, because you have a partner who doesn't want to make you feel good. Your relationship is in serious trouble.

Remember that at the top of the relationship pyramid (see page xiv) is the challenge to do one thing each day that makes your partner feel good about themselves. A partner who puts you down is doing the exact opposite. Consequently, the product of relationship disrespect is a chronic feeling of undesirability—that you have nothing to offer or aren't attractive or smart enough to be of any value.

It isn't unreasonable to want your partner to be aware of how their actions impact your psyche. So if you make it clear that certain things are hurtful and the pattern still continues, you'll have to make a difficult decision regarding the real worth of this relationship. It isn't any fun to be with a partner who doesn't want to spend any time with you—but it's even more painful to have a partner who *is* around you but does things to make you feel bad. The only outcome will be many days of arguments, and eventually, loneliness. You shouldn't have to "toughen up" to handle a partner who doesn't care about your happiness. You deserve better than that.

The Next Step

I know that this chapter contains a lot of information for you to digest, but I hope that it will help you categorize your emotions and allow you to see the basis for most of the arguments you have with your partner. The next time you feel angry after a conflict with your partner, ask yourself, "What is this really about? Did I not get what I really wanted? Did I not get heard? Did my partner get lazy and do nothing about the problem? Did my feelings get hurt?"

The tips in this chapter will be tremendously helpful in putting you on the road to successful conflict management. You will have opened the door so that you and your partner can have a constructive discussion on the specifics of the situation.

Now we need to go on to the next logical step in becoming a great relationship problem solver. After the conflict is put out on the table for open discussion, you must both then enter into a process of negotiation and compromise. I know this sounds more like a business proposition, but it's really about the *business* of your intimate relationship.

CHAPTER 3

THE ART OF NEGOTIATION AND COMPROMISE

One of the questions I'm asked most frequently in interviews is: "What's the most important skill for a couple to develop to ensure a great relationship?" I always answer in the same way: "The ability to rationally negotiate through a problem and then reach a fair compromise that both people can accept."

As I said in the last chapter, negotiation and compromise form the grunt work of a relationship—there's nothing romantic about it. But this is **Step 3** in solving relationship problems, and it simply cannot be overlooked . . . or it will lead to bigger problems down the road.

You'll probably never experience the pressure of negotiating a multimillion-dollar merger or a hostage situation, but you'll certainly feel the strain of a relationship on the brink of collapse if you don't try to perfect these important skills. So let's first define the terms and then see how they actually play out over the course of a relationship.

What Is a Negotiation?

The best way I can illustrate a negotiation is to break it down like this:

You and your partner have a problem——▶ you find a way to solve it——▶ your problem is resolved.

This is a pretty simple schematic, but it works. *Negotiation* is actually a rather broad term, since it can lead to a really bad outcome for one side, a really good outcome for one side, or a fair resolution for both. It could encompass a screaming match, silence, or a rational discussion of your problem—it's merely the process you and your partner utilize, whether productive for, or destructive to, the relationship. (But if you do use destructive tactics and you don't seek to modify them, you're going to end up having an attorney negotiate your divorce settlement.)

Most of the time you probably don't even notice when you negotiate with your partner. My goal in this section is to at least make you aware of the fact that most of your relationship behaviors are *some* type of a negotiation.

For instance, if your partner yells, "Shut up!" and you scream back, "I'll talk whenever I want!" you've just negotiated the frequency of your communication. If your partner makes a nasty remark about the dinner you just cooked and you start to cry and leave the room, you've negotiated a settlement for yourself that it's better to break down instead of face criticism. Neither of these negotiations will lead to productive solutions, but they're both negotiations nevertheless.

Negotiation also comes in handy when you and your partner want or need different things: He wants to vacation on the beach; you want to go skiing in the mountains. She wants a big family of eight children; you want to remain childless. He wants to go out with friends after work every night; you want to stay home. You get the picture.

The key point for you to remember is that a negotiation goes much more smoothly when both parties can sit down and talk in a calm and reasonable manner. Here are a few examples of poor negotiation tactics:

- Playing hardball in order to absolutely have it your own way, without regard to your partner's feelings

- Yelling and screaming

- Storming out of the room when things get heated, or avoiding the issue altogether

- Refusing to listen to your partner's point of view

Clearly, these techniques just won't cut it. However, if you remember this little caveat, you'll be well on your way: *A good negotiator listens more than he or she talks in order to understand the other person's point of view.* Whether you ultimately agree with their position is another matter, but the process of listening will be what really counts.

So the next time you and your mate have a disagreement, really listen to what they have to say, and then seek to understand their motives (no matter how crazy they may seem). Only then can you make the following statement, which is the hallmark of a good negotiator: "I really want to understand where you're coming from. Here's how *I* feel about ____ [the issue at hand]."

After you've shared with your partner, back off and listen to their response. Hopefully you have a partner who's also invested in a good negotiation, so there can be a satisfactory conclusion to the problem. (Don't worry—we'll discuss the partner who's not interested in listening to your side of things in the next chapter.) Negotiation and compromise must be a two-way street—if one partner chooses not to play, then the relationship will suffer.

What Is a Compromise?

The word *compromise* should become the single most important word in your relationship vocabulary. I've personally known couples who had a lot in common, a great sex life, and undying love for each other . . . but a complete inability to compromise. Consequently, the relationship fell apart.

Here's the difference between negotiation and compromise: Negotiation is the actual process of trying to figure out a solution to your relationship problem, and compromise *is* that solution. In other words, negotiating (talking) has to be done because you have a certain need that doesn't agree with your partner's different need. In the best-case scenario, a solution is reached in which you both give up something yet enter into a situation that's best for the relationship in general. This is the beauty of a compromise—both partners work as a team to claim the real victory, and the relationship subsequently prospers.

Now you may be thinking that a compromise is then defined as a 50-50 split on every decision. But in practical terms, it just isn't possible to always do it 50 percent your way and 50 percent your partner's way. For example, on weekends my wife, Betsy, and I have very different agendas—I want to watch sports, and she wants to run errands or go shopping with me. This one is easy—the

50-percent split actually works well here—because for half the day I get to do what I want, and for the other half of the day we do what she wants. An even compromise is struck.

But in another problem area, the percentage has to be modified. You see, Betsy usually drives many more miles on a daily basis than I do, so during bad weather she really needs a larger and safer vehicle. This means that I then get stuck driving a smaller car, which I don't like or enjoy, but I do it for her safety. So in this case, there really is no even compromise—I give in, and it's 100 percent her way and zero percent my way.

This example nicely illustrates one of the main points regarding a good compromise—that is, sometimes you'll have to completely give in and not get your way at all. But this is still a compromise because there's a give-and-take. Perhaps on another issue down the road I'll get to have it *all* my way and my wife will make a compromise for me. I'm thinking that I'll never have to do any housework ever again and that she'll completely agree with me on this one (just kidding!). That's one compromise that won't happen in my lifetime, but I can always hope. . . .

Before I summarize the principles of a good compromise, please allow me to digress just briefly because this is really important. The reality is this—you're not a child anymore; therefore, you can't expect your partner to cater to your every whim. Children throw tantrums and pout when they don't get their way—adults need to face the fact that we can't always get what they want.

So one of the first compromises you must make with yourself is the following (and say this out loud so it really sinks in): *I can't always have my way. Sometimes I'll have to give in even if I think I'm right. I'll try to do my fair share in the relationship to make it successful, and I won't be lazy and expect my partner to do all of the work.*

If you're able to make and follow this internal compromise with yourself, then you'll head off many potential problems at the pass. Now let's outline several principles that you can follow when negotiating a compromise that will work for you both.

The Real Way to Solve Any Relationship Problem

Here are several things that must happen in order for a relationship issue to be resolved. I want you to refer back to these principles as you read about specific problems listed in each chapter because the process is the same.

Remember, **Step 1** in solving a relationship conflict is always the commitment to stop yelling at and berating each other in the course of talking about the problem—you must both agree to respect each other's opinions. **Step 2** is actually identifying the issue and then telling your partner your specific complaint and how you feel. These two steps must be done first, or the process of negotiating some kind of compromise will be meaningless.

When you're ready to move on to **Step 3**, there are several core principles that must be adhered to. They're detailed below.

Principle #1: You and your partner should never keep a running tally of "wins" and "losses" in your negotiations.

Sadly, this is one of the biggest mistakes that I see couples make. Believe me, most people won't admit this out loud, but they're keeping score internally, just waiting for the day they finally get to "win." When you hear your partner (or yourself) complain, "You always get your way. It's *my* turn now!" it's time to realize that score *is* being kept.

Why shouldn't you keep track of victories and losses so that over time things are evened up? It would only make sense to win an argument sometimes, and I'll grant you that your relationship should be an equal partnership. The problem with keeping score is that the win-loss record usually becomes the most important factor in resolving a dispute, rather than the need to figure out each issue on its own merit. A friend of mine once proudly told me that he'd gotten his way four times that week, compared to his wife getting her way only twice. He didn't care if he was right or wrong, just as long as he got in the last word and won the argument. Giving in for him meant that he was somehow "weak" and losing control. Although I thought he was completely insane (and I told him so), I tried to make him understand that this behavior would only serve to drive a wedge in his marriage and make his wife disgusted with his competitiveness.

Compromise is *not* a sign of personal weakness. It's really okay to let your partner come out on top sometimes. This can be an extremely hard thing to do, but challenge yourself to wipe the slate clean before you tackle a new relationship issue. If you're being hardheaded and are only interested in evening up the score, then you won't be able to see the problem clearly, and a very bad decision could be made that irreversibly harms your relationship.

Principle #2: The language you use toward your partner is critically important in determining the outcome of any problem.

Even though you may be right, you may not get your way if your method of communicating isn't effective. It will do you no good to put your partner on the defensive right away with accusatory language. When someone's being attacked, it's a natural defense mechanism for them to either fight back or retreat into a shell—in either case, the problem won't be rationally solved.

Here are a few examples of language choices that will get you nowhere fast:

— *Using the words <u>always</u> and <u>never</u>.* Saying something like, "You *never* help out around here!" or "You *always* put other people ahead of me!" will stop any reasonable discussion dead in its tracks. It sounds like you're exaggerating, and your partner will invariably be challenged to fight back in their defense. They'll probably respond with something like, "That's not true! Remember that time two weeks ago that I helped clean up the house and took the kids to school . . . " It turns into a "he said, she said" debate, and the real issue gets lost in the translation.

So catch yourself when you use words that imply absolutes. Using the above examples, it would be better to start off by saying, "I'd like to talk to you about your share of the workload," and "I'd really like it if you put me first—sometimes I feel second to your friends, relatives, and co-workers."

— *Insults and name-calling.* Some of us grew up believing that the more belligerent and loud we were, the more we'd command attention. Nothing could be further from the truth. Sure, this technique may intimidate and belittle your partner into compliance, but you'll also make them angry and resentful of your ways. They might not have the guts to tell you to your face, but they'll secretly feel that you're a real jerk.

Every time you or your partner call each other "stupid" or an "idiot" or an even nastier slur, a little bit of your relationship gets destroyed in the process. On top of that, your original problem will get lost in a barrage of obscenities, and nothing gets solved. So if you're being insulted, the right move is to say, as calmly as you can, "I can't continue to talk to you right now if you're going to use that language," and then offer to pick up the conversation later when your partner has calmed down. If they continue to aggressively come at you, then you need to question whether you'll be able to stay in a relationship with someone who's that emotionally and verbally abusive.

— *Saying "or else!"* A lot of people I know love to tack this little threat at the end of a command— for example, "You better do things my way, or else!" Apparently they feel as if their need will get met more quickly if there's a hint of some consequence. But the real question should be: "Or else what?" What will you really do if your partner ignores your request? How will you retaliate? The problem with this choice of words is that very few people respond favorably to a threat and will actually do the opposite just to show that they won't be coerced into a specific action. Your bluff may be called, and then what will you be prepared to do? If you back down, then your threat is meaningless.

Instead, think through your response very carefully and tell your partner, "Here's what I'm going to do if you don't respond to me." It's certainly okay to provide a consequence if your partner fails to correct a problem in the relationship, but that consequence needs to be well defined.

So how can you ensure that you'll actually get heard? There are better ways to communicate your desires, as shown by the following few examples that can apply to any relationship problem:

- "I'd like it if we could take some time today to talk about something that's really important to me."

- "I feel that this is a problem we can work together on."

- "This is really difficult for me to bring up, but I just want to tell you how I feel about . . . "

- "I just need you to listen and try to reserve judgment until I'm finished."

- "I'm just asking you to hear what I'm saying—we don't have to fix the problem right this second."

Principle #3: You'll have more success by focusing on one issue at a time.

One of my biggest challenges during couples therapy is to keep the two people from veering off into too many directions at once. It's nearly impossible to analyze more than one major issue at a time, which is why problem solving often fails miserably. Recently my wife and I started to discuss some money-management issues, and before we knew it, we ended the conversation by debating the amount of time we spend together. We caught our mistake and got back to the topic of money, but it did take some effort.

Make a commitment to actively focus on *one thing at a time.* I know it sounds difficult, but the payoff will be well worth the extra effort. Be aware, though, that your partner may try to derail the discussion by veering onto another topic if things start to get heated—it's a sneaky little tactic to shift the conversation when things aren't going so well. So every time you catch your partner avoiding the topic at hand, say, "Let's continue to deal with _____ now and get to _____ [the other issue] later."

Principle #4: Set the right stage for the discussion and negotiation of the problem.

There's a correct time and place to work on your problems. Let's deal with *place* first.

I can't tell you the exact room of your house that will work best for you, but a good rule of thumb is that it should be a location that's both quiet and comfortable—maybe it's your kitchen table or your den . . . it just shouldn't be in public or at a friend's home. Major discussions deserve to be held in a consistent, appropriate location. Forgetting to set the scene is a crucial blunder made by a lot of couples, so put some thought into this.

The right *time* for the negotiation is just as important as place. I believe that there are three important considerations in this area:

First, you must (and I can't stress the word *must* enough) point out a problem the *very first time* it arises. You'll have more leverage if you don't allow something to snowball into a pattern of behavior. Many people finally put their foot down when their partner has made a major mistake for about the 32nd time, but by then it's simply too late. The reality is this: The longer you allow your partner to get away with unacceptable behavior, the harder it will be to have any power to get them to stop. If you hold your tongue and just hope that your partner will change on their own, don't complain that you never get what you need.

Second, make sure that you have enough time available to thoroughly discuss the problem. Some of my patients will bring up an extremely important issue right before our time is up for the session and then get angry when I say that we have to stop. The same principle applies to your relationship: If you and your partner begin to argue just as you're leaving for work or getting ready to go out, then the discussion will be nonproductive. Alternately, if you put off the issue too long, you run the risk that the problem will never be solved. So set aside an appropriate length of time for a face-to-face meeting (notice that a phone conversation is generally not intimate enough).

Third, when you and your partner have been sitting there for hours still hammering away without a compromise, it may be time to call it quits for the time being and readdress the problem again later. When you both get tired and start to go 'round and 'round, it's acceptable to say, "How about if we agree to disagree for now and pick up our discussion later when we're both fresh?"

Principle #5: Say "I'm sorry" if you act in a disrespectful or hurtful way toward your partner.

This one is short and sweet. You're not perfect—once in a while you may unintentionally (or intentionally) hurt your partner's feelings. You may say mean-spirited things in the heat of the moment that you immediately regret—so swallow your pride, apologize, and ask for forgiveness. By the same token, you should also expect an "I'm sorry" from your partner if *your* feelings were hurt by disrespectful behavior.

I know there's a chance that you had parents who abused each other and became overwhelmed by relationship problems, and I'll bet that they rarely said they were sorry for their actions. So be different—become truly free in your relationship by admitting that you were wrong. Really value your partner, and don't let *your* relationship have an unhappy ending.

◆ ◆ ◆

You're now armed with some very important negotiating and compromising skills to use in any disagreement; and by utilizing these techniques, you'll have much greater success in solving difficult relationship problems.

But I also know that sometimes you and your partner will reach an impasse. If the first attempt to reach a solution is unsuccessful, then what? What will you do if things don't significantly change? In the next chapter, I'll teach you how to determine whether the problem is really gone, or conversely, what to do if your partner doesn't listen and breaks promises. This will be **Step 4** in handling relationship conflicts.

CHAPTER 4

AN END TO THE ARGUMENTS

How do you know when an argument is really over? Unfortunately for most couples, discussions end when one person storms out of the room, one freezes the other out with the old silent treatment, or one yells, "That's just the way it's gonna be!" Clearly, even though that particular exchange may have ended, the problem is far from being solved.

This chapter starts with the following truth: *The talking may have stopped, but that doesn't mean that the problem has gone away!*

It's certainly no fun to hash out difficult relationship problems. That's why many of us fall into the common trap of arguing without first defining the answers to the following:

Question #1: What am I truly fighting over? In other words, have I strictly defined what I need?

Question #2: What specific outcome must result so I feel that the problem-solving attempt has been successful?

Few of your problems will ever be resolved to your sat-isfaction if you're not disciplined enough to ask these questions of yourself each and every time a conflict arises in your relationship—no matter whether you're living together, married, or just dating. Unless you've first figured out how you want the conflict to be resolved, your discussion will have no chance of reaching a satisfactory con-clusion (for either of you). And isn't the goal of any dis-cussion to reach a reasonable end point so that you can go on to other enjoyable activities that will enhance the relationship?

Possible Solutions

Let's take a look at the outcomes that will result from an attempt to solve a relationship problem. One of these scenarios obviously represents the best result, while the other two will mean that further action is warranted.

Outcome #1: The problem goes away!

Congratulations! You and your partner have success-fully completed the first three steps aimed at solving your problem: You both agreed to behave in a rational and calm manner and didn't berate each other during the dis-cussion (**Step 1**); you each specifically defined the actual problem and how you felt (**Step 2**); and you were able to negotiate a solution and then reach a compromise that enhanced the relationship (**Step 3**). Both of you can now walk away with a feeling of victory, since a fair decision was reached. **Step 4** has now been accomplished—and the argument is over for good! You defined your needs and the desired outcome, and success is yours.

How do you know if the problem will ever rear its ugly head again? Ultimately, only time will tell whether it's truly gone forever. For example, if you ask your partner to spend more time with the children and this is done consistently, then everyone's a winner; if you ask for more romance and things consistently heat up in the bedroom, then the relationship has improved. Of course, the key determining factor here is the *consistency* of your partner's response. You should be able to assume that the offending behavior will never be repeated again—or if there *is* an occasional slip-up, it's quickly admitted to and corrected. It may not be reasonable in every case to expect that the problem will never, ever arise again, but you can take comfort in the fact that the overall pattern has been broken.

Outcome #2: The problem gets better for a while, but then it reappears.

Sadly enough, this is the category that most relationship issues end up in. You may have followed every step correctly—you defined the point of contention, the negotiation went smoothly, and the problem went away—but what do you do if your partner goes back on their word and falls into the old way of behaving?

You must quickly and aggressively jump on the issue again before it gets out of hand. If you don't respond, you'll be in violation of a major rule of problem solving: *The longer you let a problem go unchecked, the harder it will be to eradicate it!* This means that the very second a promise is broken, you should attempt to take immediate corrective action. This approach may sound extreme to you, and you may hear such protests as, "Hey, get off my back!" But your reply should be: *"You're* the one who broke your promise to abide by our original solution."

Now this doesn't necessarily mean that an issue can never be revisited or an updated plan be put into effect. Sometimes circumstances change—maybe your financial picture is different now and you need to adjust your original response to a conflict over money; perhaps because of a new job, your time situation has shifted and the household duties need to be split up differently. That's certainly okay, but you need to deal with it right away.

The bottom line here is that everyone has the tendency to fall back into familiar ruts and return to old, nonproductive ways of doing things. It's just human nature to try to sneak back to the way that feels comfortable and easy. But this shouldn't stop you from demanding that your partner absolutely follow the spirit of the original solution that you reached together.

Before we move on to the next outcome, I must address two other aspects of a broken promise. First, there are certain promises that can *never*, under any circumstances, be broken—not even once. Ask yourself, "What values do I hold so sacred that, if they're broken by my partner, will absolutely lead to the immediate dissolution of our relationship?"

Before you're backed into a corner during the heat of battle, sit down and decide which actions are "relationship-enders" versus those things that are harmful to the relationship but deserve another chance to be corrected. That way, you'll already have your answer during those critical times when you must decide whether to stay in the relationship or go. (Perhaps you have an absolute prohibition against divorce and believe that you should stay in a marriage—no matter how destructive it is—for "better or worse." If that's the case, you probably don't need to make this list, because your partner could do just about anything to you and you'll take it. I think that's a shame, but you may have a religious or moral belief that precludes you from moving on.)

As we proceed here, I'd like you to list what I call your "sacred needs" relating to each chapter's topic. I can't choose these for you—no one can define what you will and will not tolerate except you! As for me, if my wife cheated on me, spent all of our money without my permission, was physically abusive, or absolutely refused to get any professional help if we were struggling—these would certainly be relationship-enders for me—that is, they'd be a violation of my sacred needs. But my values and yours may be entirely different, so it's up to you to define your own limits.

Also keep in mind that there are many problems that fall in the "in-between" category—they won't necessarily cause you to end the relationship, but they must be immediately addressed. The question you should ask yourself is: "How many times can my partner make this mistake before there's a serious consequence?" For instance, let's say that your partner has the tendency to call you derogatory names during arguments, and you say that this is unacceptable. They agree to stop, yet keep doing it over and over again. What's your limit—1 more time, 2 more times . . . 36 more times? If this behavior isn't on your list of relationship-enders, how many screw-ups will you allow before serious action is taken? Think about how many times you'll forgive your partner for the same transgression if there's no serious attempt to stop. Then stick to your guns.

Outcome #3: Your partner ignores your needs and makes no attempt to really solve the problem.

Some people think that nothing is ever their fault and assign the blame for their problems on everyone else. This is narcissism in its purest form, and it makes for terrible, destructive relationships that will never reach their full potential. Not only will a partner like this wreck your self-esteem, they'll also eventually tear apart any sense of a good relationship.

The most obvious manifestation of this poor coping skill is denial that the relationship is in trouble. I've known people who simply refused to modify their behavior—even when their partner is practically begging for their cooperation. So you need to ask yourself, "What will I do if my partner ignores my needs and does nothing to work out our problems?"

There are two different ways in which your partner may ignore a troubling situation that simply must be addressed. First, you may be met with a string of "I'll get to it" responses. No matter how much you ask for some action, nothing productive occurs. Your partner just keeps on doing the same thing without regard to your feelings. Second, if your problems have gotten so bad that you need some professional help, your partner may absolutely refuse to see someone with you, insisting that you have to figure it out on your own. On my radio show, I've heard several stories about men who just won't go to any sort of therapy even if they cheat on, or are physically abusive to, their wives. They'll say, "We don't have any problems!" and then will continue to repeat the same destructive behaviors. These guys have no motivation whatsoever to change in any meaningful way.

So let's go back to my original question: What will you do if your partner doesn't care enough to alter a certain behavior? This is critical now, because the ball is actually in your court. Once you know that your partner refuses to discuss certain issues, won't act on any reasonable suggestions, or won't listen to you, there's a decision to be made—by *you*. What will your next step be? Here are your nonproductive options:

- Do nothing, drop the subject, and be miserable.

- Make idle threats such as, "I'm going to leave you this time!" or "You better shape up or else!" and then stay in the relationship and act as if nothing has happened.

- Complain to anyone who will listen that your partner is mean and disrespectful. A lot of us engage in this little exercise in futility—it accomplishes nothing, but we get a lot of sympathy. Again, your partner will have little incentive to really look at the problem seriously.

There is one other possibility, the one that I feel will work best for you and your relationship in the long run. It isn't the most pleasant or comfortable position to take, but ultimately it *will* lead to a conclusion—either the offending behavior will stop, or you'll be able to remove yourself from the situation.

First, ask yourself if you're willing to leave the relationship over the conflict or your partner's refusal to change. If the answer to this question is yes, then there's only one option for you. It's time to draw a line in the sand and say, *"This is all I'm willing to take, and if things don't change now, I need to leave this relationship."* Memorize this line, because someday you may need to say it, exactly as written. But here's the catch—if you *do* say this to your partner, then you better mean it. It's the only leverage you'll have, so you can't afford to back down and get walked over again.

I know that taking a stand like this is incredibly hard to do, since most of us don't want our relationships to fail.

I've heard the following argument countless times: "But I love him (or her)!" I'd like to point out that your most loving gestures should be to *yourself* first. How is someone showing you love if they won't even try to find solutions to problems or listen to your feelings? That's not love—it's selfishness.

It's time to take charge of your life. I challenge you to finally ask yourself this tough question: "How much pain and sadness will I endure just to be in a relationship?" I hope that you have the strength to stand up for your beliefs; and the courage to move on if all avenues of decency, respect, and kindness have been closed in your relationship. After all, your life shouldn't be filled with problems that just won't go away. You can do better.

◆ ◆ ◆

Congratulations on completing the first part of the book and learning the mechanics of how to solve virtually any relationship problem! I hope that you'll apply these general principles to every conflict that arises in your love relationships. If you need to, reread the material up to this point and get a firm grasp on the four steps to conflict resolution. Believe it or not, yelling and screaming at each other is the easy thing to do—making a sincere attempt to change things is a lot harder.

I don't know if there's one secret to making a love relationship stand the test of time, but I do know this—your search for peace and harmony must begin with the courage to do something different if what you're currently doing isn't making you happy. Remember this truth: *If something isn't working for you, you must put forth the effort to change it!* It simply won't change by itself. Problem solving takes energy, but that effort can pay off in huge dividends.

With that said, let's now begin the process of systematically tackling the major relationship problems that can challenge us all. Each chapter from hereon in will focus on a particular problem area, and outline real solutions that can truly work for you and your partner. Your love, marital, or dating relationship will then be the true winner.

PART II

WHAT ARE YOU FIGHTING ABOUT?

CHAPTER 5

MONEY

The reason why money is the first issue we're going to address in the second half of this book is that it's generally the number-one reason why couples break up. It seems incredible that financial problems could override love and commitment and lead to a relationship's failure, but it happens all the time.

So it's time to systematically look at the main hurdles that arise when you struggle with money management. But first, let's briefly explore the psychology of money to understand why finances are such a sensitive and explosive subject for couples to face.

What Money Means to Us

For most of us, money is our gateway to the world: having it means that we feel secure; not having it makes us feel unhappy, like we're failures. And if you've ever heard of the "Golden Rule of Relationships" (he with the most gold makes the rules), then you know that cash can equal power in relationships. Think about these questions:

1. Who will handle your money?
2. How will you spend your money?
3. How will you deal with unexpected changes in your finances?
4. Are you afraid that at any time your money could be taken away and that you'll go broke?
5. Does the breadwinner get to set all the relationship rules?

If handled correctly, the process of managing money jointly can strengthen your relationship; if handled incorrectly, money management can lead to intense arguments, hurt feelings, and a trip to bankruptcy court. So it's vitally important that you learn how to successfully deal with this issue.

The Solutions to Your Money Problems

The format for the rest of this chapter (and each successive chapter) will be as follows: I'll present a problem and then offer a solution for you to consider. And for each topic, I'll discuss what I feel are the main areas that can blow a relationship apart if not worked through by you and your partner.

I know that some of you may complain, "Well, he didn't talk about _____, and that's a huge problem for us!" Just understand that *no* book can cover every single problem that could possibly arise. I believe that the areas I present to you here are the most critical issues that arise in relationships.

What we tackled in the first part of the book can be applied to each of these chapters. That is, you and your partner should first be able to identify your problem spots and then try to compromise on a solution. Sure, it sounds really simple, but most couples lose their focus when things heat up, and then the problem has little chance of actually getting resolved.

So, let's make money management a lot easier and more organized.

Problem #1: Accounting

Most couples I know have some difficulty deciding who's going to keep track of the bills and expenditures and balance the checkbook. Now these tasks certainly aren't glamorous—in fact, they're downright tedious. That's why many of us avoid it like the plague. But *somebody* has to be the designated accountant; otherwise, your finances will be a total mess. So who's going to do it?

Solution #1

You both need to sit down and designate one person to keep track of all the money that comes in and goes out of your household. This doesn't mean that this person gets to unilaterally decide all money matters—this is just a bookkeeping function. So who's more organized, you or your partner? (This is a critical decision, so be honest.)

Once you've decided on the money manager, the other person must agree to faithfully give all receipts and records of money spent to the banker. I sure used to be guilty of violating this little rule. I'd go to the ATM, withdraw some money, and then forget to give the record to my wife (our designated banker). Of course, this behavior caused us to be off by many dollars when Betsy balanced our checkbook. Boy, was she was mad . . . and she had every right to be, because I made her job more difficult. (Thankfully, I've been trained now.)

The other side to this coin is that the banker must be open about the accounts at all times. The nonbanker should be able to see the checkbook and bank statements at any point. This minimizes the risk that someone will go crazy and spend all of the money. This leads us to our next topic for discussion.

◆ ◆ ◆

Problem #2: Spending

Recently, a friend of mine went to buy a new car. She was shocked when the salesperson told her that she had a low credit rating, and therefore wouldn't be able to qualify for a low percentage rate. My friend became infuriated and called the credit bureau to see how this could be— she was under the impression that she had very good credit. The bureau told her that she and her husband had several credit cards that were maxed out . . . which my friend knew nothing about.

That's when her husband confessed that the charges were correct. Unbeknownst to his wife, this man had opened several charge accounts and had secretly been paying off the balances. This amounted to several thousand dollars' worth of purchases, which helped amass their debt.

You may wonder how this could happen. Didn't the wife see the monthly statements arriving in the mail? Well, her husband was able to fool her because he'd had the bills sent to a post office box and had sneaked small sums of money out of their checking account each month to make the minimum payments. But the result of his behavior was their near financial ruin.

This case illustrates the fact that your partner may sometimes spend money without asking you first. Hopefully it won't be as extreme as the example above, but people *will* occasionally spend money first and ask questions later.

I go out for lunch a few times a week and don't call my wife to ask for permission first; she buys the groceries and doesn't ask me how much she's allowed to spend. Expenditures like these are usually not the problem areas. However, if I went to the track and gambled away my paycheck or wasted our money drinking at the local bar every night, then this would obviously become a major problem. Likewise, if my wife went out and bought expensive items and then overdrew our bank account, this issue would need to be addressed.

You don't want to end up in the "poorhouse" because of frivolous spending habits, so give some thought to the next solution.

Solution #2

There needs to be absolute agreement on the following: Neither partner will ever open up a bank or credit card account without the other person's knowledge.

In addition, a spending limit must be defined and adhered to. This means that either partner will only be allowed to spend up to a predetermined amount on any purchase or activity—you and your partner need to define that now. Anything over that amount, even slightly, must first be discussed and approved by both of you. For example, if your set amount is $200, and a new DVD player costs $250, then you must decide *together* whether to buy it. (Of course, emergencies arise, but that's not what we're talking about here.)

If this rule is broken, then the offending partner will do whatever it takes to make things right. If that means returning the merchandise, taking a second job to pay off the debt, or closing all of the accounts . . . then so be it. If you make the mess, you'd better be willing to clean it up.

If you find that spending has become an addiction, then you need to seek out professional help. There's always a psychological basis for out-of-control spending, and it should be addressed immediately.

◆ ◆ ◆

Problem #3: Reversal of Fortune

I'm sure you've dreamed that winning the lottery would be the answer to all your financial woes, but it's actually been shown that a good percentage of winners declare bankruptcy within a few years because they have no long-term financial goals.

Similarly, imagine that you or your partner walk into work one day and find out that you're being laid off or fired. This seems devastating and would certainly have an immediate impact on your lives, but if you've done some planning beforehand, it doesn't have to ruin your finances forever.

The lesson here is that you really don't know what life will bring you. Maybe your stocks will hit it big one day (or tank the next); perhaps you'll get an unexpected windfall from a relative's estate; or you could be out of work for several months and have to scrape by just to put food on the table. Each of these situations demands a flexible yet well-prepared response.

So how will you cope with an unexpected change in your finances (either up or down)? Here are some pointers that can save you and your partner a lot of sleepless nights.

Solution #3

I believe that the key to staying afloat financially can be found in two simple words: *Plan ahead.* I understand that you and your partner won't want to think about suddenly losing your source of income or having to spend your life savings, but in a volatile economy, these things happen more and more. So start planning for that rainy day—believe me, if you wake up one morning to find out that you have nothing left, your relationship will greatly suffer.

Begin the process of talking about money with your partner on a regular basis so that a plan is put into place to save. Here's how to start:

1. First, thoroughly break down *exactly* how much money comes in and goes out of the household on a monthly basis.

2. If you find that you have nothing left at the end of the month, then immediately start decreasing your expenditures. If you *do* have something left over, then decide how much of this will be put away in a savings account, which won't be touched for *any* reason other than an emergency. This is your "rainy-day fund."

3. Finally, both of you need to commit to learning about prudent money management by reading books, meeting with an accountant or financial planner, and/or understanding how different types of accounts work. Educate yourself—it will pay off big-time in your relationship!

◆ ◆ ◆

Problem #4: The Miser

Apparently, some people don't believe the old saying "You can't take it with you." I've treated people who literally hoard all of their money in a closet or under their bed because they're so afraid to part with any of it.

Unfortunately, this pattern usually leads to a miserable life characterized by deprivation and obsessive behavior. It also greatly affects intimate relationships, since most people want to have some fun once in a while. You and your partner deserve to enjoy the fruits of your labors sometimes, even if this means that you need to spend some money on a vacation or a new possession. This doesn't contradict my previous advice—I'm not advocating that you go crazy and blow it all at once. But there *is* a way to enjoy life *and* save at the same time.

However, you or your partner may become so consumed with money matters that one of you will refuse to spend *anything*—even on necessities. This is unfortunate, since this attitude will undoubtedly impact your relationship in negative ways. Arguments will ensue about who's spending what and how much, and who's saving the most. Keep this in mind if you're dating someone who refuses to spend any money on you . . . this may be what you get (or don't get) for the rest of your life.

So what should you do if you're with someone who constantly obsesses about money issues or who won't spend anything to enhance the relationship? Read on.

Solution #4

You first need to realize that a so-called cheapskate is playing out underlying psychological issues. Usually this dynamic is centered on the belief that holding on to money equals security. Some people find that having a lot of cash gives them a sense of accomplishment and pride.

Many of us also grew up listening to our parents argue about money. This sets up a subconscious need to value money to a fault, coupled with the fear that it will all be taken away at any moment. Consequently, money hounds will attempt to keep it for as long as they can, while protesting that it's for the "good" of the relationship.

Your first step here is to gently tell your partner that there might be other emotional reasons why they have difficulty parting with money. You may be met with the excuse, "I'm just doing it for us," but you should respond that you're unhappy and the relationship is suffering.

Next, offer to sit down and work out a compromise with respect to luxury items such as vacations, cars, nice clothes, leisure activities, and so forth. Tell your partner that you need to have some fun (and nice things) now and again—you both deserve to live a little. I choose the word *deserve* because some people seem to think that life should all be about work and sacrifice.

Finally, if time goes on and nothing changes, suggest that your partner talk to a therapist. At various points in this book, I'll suggest therapy if all other options fail, and this is one of those times. You shouldn't have to go through life worrying every second about how much is being spent. After all, an important part of a love relationship is giving, both in emotional *and* in materialistic ways.

◆ ◆ ◆

Problem #5: Money As Power

In a relationship full of sharing and fairness, it won't really matter who brings home the most money; but in a relationship filled with greed and envy, money will probably be used as the ultimate leverage to manipulate situations in a certain way.

I've known people who will withhold money if their partner doesn't do exactly what they want. It's an unspoken way of saying, "I'll let you in on the money if you give me something in return." In fact, I know of a woman who stayed in a loveless marriage for years and got bossed around by a controlling husband, but, hey, she got to drive a Mercedes and go on extravagant shopping sprees if she did exactly what he demanded.

Would you trade emotional happiness for material possessions? A lot of folks do, but I doubt that deep down inside they truly feel good about themselves.

At some point you may find yourself dealing with a partner who will use money to gain power. Not only is this completely unfair, but it will ultimately create an imbalance in the relationship. The most obvious illustration of this concept is when one partner makes a lot more money than their partner. It used to be the man who was the primary breadwinner, but more and more, that dynamic is being reversed. A good friend of mine makes more than her husband does, but they've managed to keep things equal on an emotional level. Another couple divorced because the husband made more and rubbed it in the face of his wife every time they disagreed about anything.

What makes these two couples different? Well, the successful couple followed the solution below.

Solution #5

You and your partner need to completely agree on the importance of money in your relationship: If you're in disagreement about another subject (such as children, sex, or housework), money must never be brought into the equation as a form of leverage. You never want to hear the following statement from your partner: "I won't give you any more money if you don't do what I say!" You can't allow yourself to be held hostage by a partner who exerts power through finances.

In a committed relationship, money should go into one account and be shared equally—both partners need to have the same access to it. Relationships in which the mode of operation is: "You have your money and I have mine" have a greater chance of failing. In my view, it doesn't matter if one partner makes 100 percent of the money—both of you are a team. There are many contributions to any relationship that cannot be measured in dollars and cents. Agree on this principle.

The partner making the most money doesn't get to make all the life decisions! So many couples make this mistake—the earner decides everything because the other person feels dependent and subservient. Eventually the one taking orders will become jealous, angry, and resentful and may exert power in other destructive ways. If you're the one making less than your partner, it's really okay. If you need to catch up monetarily, then do something to further your career. Also, let go of any envy you feel toward your partner, and focus on the things you *can* do.

♦ ♦ ♦

You now have practical solutions that will help you handle financial roadblocks. These problems don't have to destroy your relationship if you both agree to *talk* about them often. I truly hope that someday you'll also come to define *richness* without ever using the word *money* . . . other aspects of your relationship will seem much more important when you look back many years from now.

■ ■ ◊ O ◊ ■ ■

CHAPTER 6

SEX

Sex is a very touchy subject for most of us to talk about (no pun intended). We tend to expect romance to just magically occur without any discussion, believing on some level that our partner should just intuit what we prefer in the bedroom. Sometimes sex is great and seems effortless, but we can often end up feeling unfulfilled and disappointed.

Many times in my career I've made the following point: Sex is certainly important in relationships, but it's not the only thing that will determine your happiness—nor can it define your relationship over a long period of time.

Having said that, I do want to note that a satisfying sex life will enhance your bond *and* increase your relationship's chance of success. A couple who has great sex will be more connected and treat each other in a more loving way. The thing to remember is that intimacy—which includes *many* behaviors that go beyond the actual act of sexual intercourse—counts. Hugging, kissing, hand-holding, and exchanging love notes are all forms of intimate behavior that should be present in a healthy relationship.

In this chapter, it's my intention to offer up solutions to several major issues that impact intimate relationships. I've been talking about sexual topics in the media for more than a decade now, so I have a pretty good foundation of knowledge on the subject. I don't intend to offend you with graphic details, but a discussion like this needs to be frank. And if you're struggling with any of the following problems, I hope that you'll open up a line of dialogue with your partner—who will only know that something's wrong if you speak up.

Before we get started, I'd like to warn you not to fall into the trap of talking about sex only when you're in your bedroom or during the throes of passion. This is a bad idea, since the conversation will inevitably take on an emotional tone when you need complete objectivity. (Of course, it's all right to guide your partner during sex by telling them that something feels good, but don't initiate a discussion on serious sexual problems at this point.) Compatible couples talk about their needs outside of the bedroom—that is, they pick a quiet time and place, sit face-to-face with each other, and try to solve the issues in a reasonable way. It's sometimes awkward, but you must set any sense of embarrassment aside and talk about what you really want.

Let's look at some sexual problems that can make you feel very dissatisfied.

Problem #1:
Believing That Great Sex = A Great Relationship

I don't want to stereotype the genders here, but it's been proven repeatedly that women equate sex to love more so than men. In fact, many women need to feel that there's the potential for a long-term relationship before they'll even think about having sex.

Men, on the other hand, can and will copulate with someone just for the pleasure derived from the act itself. Naturally, some men need to feel a special connection, but others are able to have great sex with women they don't really care that much about. These guys can move on without looking back.

Women are often left wondering why their relationships ended after weeks or months of awesome sex. The reality is that a few nights of sex does not automatically lead to a committed, monogamous relationship.

Solution #1

You need to accept the fact that a great relationship will be based on more than sparks in the bedroom. Just because someone wants to have sex with you doesn't mean that they also want to spend the rest of their life with you. Realize that different people have different motivations for having sex—for example, they enjoy the physicality of it, they need to feel "wanted" for a brief period of time, they use sex as a tool to draw you in, and so on. There are many more psychological reasons that drive sexual behavior, but suffice it to say that not all of them are honorable.

So wise up about the meaning of sex in a relationship. After all, many couples are able to enjoy hot, passionate nights of steamy romance, only to argue and fight their way through the rest of the relationship. It's difficult for them to see things clearly because "We're having great sex!" Hold out for the entire package—a wonderful sexual experience *and* a great nonsexual partnership with your mate.

♦ ♦ ♦

Problem #2: Inability to Achieve Orgasm

Again, this problem used to be stereotypically thought of as a female one. However, there *are* men who can engage in sexual activity and never reach the point of orgasm. This is less common than the reverse case in which the man ejaculates too quickly, but it can still present a problem.

No matter which partner this issue affects, it's incredibly frustrating for both people and can lead to tension in the relationship. The first person starts thinking, *Why can't I have an orgasm? There has to be something seriously wrong,* while the other thinks, *I'm not satisfying my partner enough if they can't climax when we have sex.*

The orgasm has come to represent the benchmark of a mutually satisfying sexual experience, yet I believe that sex doesn't have to end with an orgasm. I've debated this point with many colleagues and friends who feel that orgasms are a must, but my opinion remains the same: By only focusing attention and energy on the end result (the orgasm), you and your partner may miss out on other important parts of sex, such as foreplay and just being together. Of course that's not to say that you shouldn't shoot for a great orgasm—the point is that by thinking about it too much, you'll decrease your chances of achieving one.

So what should you do if you or your partner find it difficult to fully enjoy sex? After all, both people deserve to achieve the ultimate pleasure in their sex life, even if one partner reaches an orgasm more readily.

Solution #2

I'm going to list the most common reasons why some people are unable to climax during sex. After each point, we'll look at a potential solution that may work for you or your partner.

— *Primary anorgasmia.* This means that you've never had an orgasm, even through masturbation. There are a small number of people who just cannot reach the point of orgasm, no matter what technique is used. So the first question to ask is whether you've *ever* had an orgasm. If you don't know what an orgasm feels like, there are several books that describe the experience in great detail—read up on it.

Next, see your gynecologist or urologist to rule out any medical problems. There are conditions (such as diabetes, uterine or penile problems, thyroid complications, or depression) that can lessen the ability to have an orgasm. If your doctor clears you, then it's time to examine psychological causes. Baggage from your childhood, unpleasant sexual experiences, and other inhibitions can make you anorgasmic, and therapy can certainly help you deal with these issues and enhance your sexual experience.

— *You're not properly stimulated during sex.* This is probably the most common reason for not achieving an orgasm. The bottom line is that the right parts of you must be stimulated with the right amount of touch—if this doesn't happen, you probably won't climax. And believe it or not, intercourse can actually get in the way! You or your partner may need other forms of stimulation to finally let go enough to achieve orgasm. Generally speaking, for a woman the clitoris needs to be stimulated, for it's the spot that has the greatest chance of producing an orgasm. (The clitoris is located at the top of the vaginal opening on the outside and looks like a small, round, raised area.) For a man, the penis needs the right frequency of stimulation with some lubrication.

So how will your partner know what to do? The answer is simple—you need to *tell* or *show* them what feels good. If *you* can bring yourself to orgasm, then your partner should be able to replicate the same technique for you. This leads to the third cause.

— *Your partner is unwilling to do what it takes to help you reach orgasm.* Some people are really selfish, and others just aren't gifted in the sexual arena and have poor form and technique, but you can overcome these obstacles. You need to be with someone who's willing to learn, and to take the time to improve things for *both* of you. What this means on a practical level is that if your partner climaxes first, they'll continue to do whatever is necessary to help you orgasm. However, if they consistently won't work with you, that's a big problem, which encompasses more than just sex—it's a symptom of disrespect and selfishness.

— *You can't relax enough during sex to let go.* Sex can be anxiety-provoking, especially if you're with a new partner or have various hang-ups about your body. In addition, stressors related to work or children can impact your moods and make it difficult for you to relax. Whatever the case, your anxiety level can tremendously affect your ability to have an orgasm.

The first thing to do is to identify any potential causes of nervousness and then attempt to put them aside while you have sex. I know this is easier said than done, but here's a great technique that's useful for many people. First, see if you can answer this question: "What should I be thinking about during the actual lovemaking session?" The answer is one word: "Nothing." Really try to put everything out of your head, and only focus on the sensations in your body. Successful orgasms come about after you relax enough to let it happen, which means that you may not have your best orgasms with a new partner. As you start to feel more comfortable with your partner (and practice makes perfect!), you'll increase the odds of a pleasurable outcome.

— *You just don't want to have sex at that particular moment.* You may be tired, angry at your partner, or just not in the mood for sex. That's okay. Give yourself and your partner a break and try again on another day. No one can climax every time they have sex . . . so enjoy whatever *does* happen.

Finally, remember that if you and your partner just can't get in synch, then it may be time for a trip to your friendly sex therapist or counselor. Don't be ashamed—this could be quite helpful and get you back on the right track.

♦ ♦ ♦

Problem #3: Sex-Drive Discrepancies

In an ideal world, you and your partner would want to have sex at exactly the same frequency: If you want sex three times a day, your partner would agree; if your partner wanted sex once a month, this would be fine with you, too. Unfortunately, things don't tend to be that neat in the world of sex, and people naturally desire different amounts. This can lead to big problems as feelings get hurt and egos get stepped on.

This isn't gender specific—some people may be satisfied with virtually no sex in the relationship, while others need sex almost every day (and sometimes multiple times in the same day).

Why is there such a discrepancy in sex drives from person to person? Science has yet to come up with a good explanation, except to say that it's probably a combination of genetics and psychology. So what can you do?

Solution #3

You and your partner absolutely need to discuss the sex-drive issue, because sexual frustration is one of the main reasons why people go for days without talking or even begin to cheat on each other. There's no right or wrong answer to how often you should have sex—for some couples it may be every day, and for others it may be every year—but you should both somewhat agree on the frequency. So the solution to this problem can actually be stated in steps that build on themselves:

— *Step 1.* You need to make every reasonable attempt to be with a partner who shares a sex-drive level close to yours. (If you don't believe in premarital sex, then this will be a bit difficult to determine,

since you won't know what naturally feels right.)
When you start to have sex with someone, ask
yourself if their level of desire generally matches
yours. For example, a friend of mine wanted to
have sex several times a week, yet he dated a person who thought that once a month was appropriate. Everything else was great—they had similar
interests and loved to be together—but the sex
issue ultimately ended the relationship.

— *Step 2:* Take action if your or your partner's
sex drive significantly changes during the course
of your relationship. When people lose family
members; have children; or experience financial,
health, or family problems, their sex drive can be
affected. So you need to openly discuss, and really
try to understand, why your partner is having difficulty with sex. Remember that sex is usually the
first thing to go when there are other problems not
being worked through.

Next, back off a bit and stop trying to guilt-trip
your partner into having sex with you more often.
This is difficult to do when you really desire fre-
quent intercourse, but keep in mind that pressuring someone to have sex with you will *never* lead
to good sex. (However, you should set a reasonable
timetable with your partner to resolve the problem—if it goes on too long, you both should seek
therapy.)

— *Step 3:* This is a controversial stance, but
I believe that if the rest of the relationship is fulfilling, you may need to have sex every once in a
while even if you aren't totally into it at that particular moment. You can do this occasionally to

please your partner and make them happy. Part of maintaining a relationship is the realization that at times you may have to give in to your partner. Of course, this compromise then needs to be appreciated by your partner and reciprocated in the future.

◆ ◆ ◆

Problem #4: Different Sexual Tastes

I once counseled a woman who felt badgered by her husband to perform oral sex, which was a practice that repulsed her. Unfortunately, this became an issue that threatened their entire relationship because her husband wanted fellatio desperately and told her that he'd go elsewhere to get it if she didn't comply. They were at a real impasse because neither one wanted to back down.

Another time I treated a man whose wife told him that she wanted to join a swingers' club and bring other people into their sex lives "just to add some excitement." He was shocked and felt that his wife was just looking for a way to legally cheat on him. This caused a huge rift in their relationship, and they almost split up because of it.

These two examples illustrate that there may be a major disagreement between partners with respect to what they each want and are willing to do sexually. If the behavior is illegal, physically/emotionally harmful, or obviously destructive to the relationship in general, then the decision should be easy: *Don't do it*. However, many sexual practices fall into a gray area—they're important to one partner and unattractive to the other. So how do you navigate through the problem of sexual practices that turn you off, weighed against the problem of hurting your partner's feelings when you say no?

Solution #4

Most of us just hop into bed and don't ask questions—later we find out that our partner enjoys certain sexual behaviors that completely turn us off. Either way, it's a lose-lose situation: If you refuse to do something that makes you uncomfortable, your partner will be mad; if you *do* agree, then your principles will be compromised and you may even feel used.

So it's your responsibility to find out sooner than later exactly what your partner enjoys in the bedroom—you need to talk about it and ask specific questions! This may not be the best topic for a first date, but you won't want to be unpleasantly surprised months or years later when your partner asks you to have sex with someone else while he or she watches, for example.

You also need to make it crystal clear what you will and will not do sexually. (There's no use holding back this information so that you won't offend someone—it will only lead to bigger problems down the road.) If your partner ignores your sexual boundaries, then this is a sign of disrespect. I know people who will bring up the "taboo topic" once every few months, after their partner has said no repeatedly. This is not only rude, but it's tiring as well. It's perfectly acceptable to tell your partner to back off and concentrate on the positives instead of what they're not getting.

Finally, if you've been up front and clear on your sexual "do's and don'ts" and your partner still insists on trying the unacceptable behaviors, then sex is being used as a means of control and intimidation. This is usually a sign of other bad things to come. Moreover, if your partner uses the old excuse for cheating that "I had to get it somewhere else since you wouldn't do it for me," you're better off ending this relationship as soon as you can.

Problem #5: Boring Sex

No matter how hard we try, sex can sometimes get a bit routine. I've met couples who have sex only at certain times of the day, and only in the same positions. Then they complain that their sex life seems more like work. Of course it does—imagine doing the same task in the same way day after day without any change in routine. It's enough to make you want to abstain completely.

In addition, when people get involved in a committed relationship, they start to live out new "roles" in life. This happens to everyone and can impact your relationship happiness. Now you're not just a fun-loving, sexual creature—you're also a mother, father, boss, employee, and responsible member of the community. These roles, while necessary, invariably change your self-image. Your sexual being can assume less importance, and you'll begin to see yourself as an average person. Once you lose the sense that you're a sensual man or woman, things can start to go downhill fast—you stop wearing sexy underwear and even let yourself go physically. Sex becomes a chore, not an experience filled with romance and spontaneity. A valuable connection with your partner gets lost.

Solution #5

Your sex life will only be as boring as you allow it to be. I challenge you right now to start seeing yourself as a sexual person who has the right to feel love and romance again. I don't care if you think you're ugly or overweight—you can have great sex again if you're willing to take a chance and go for it.

Remember that wonderful sex can only come about as a result of a healthy relationship, yet it can also make you feel more connected and strengthen your relationship bond—it's a two-way street. The first thing you need to do is focus on romance *outside* of the bedroom. This means that you and your partner will have to begin the process of reconnecting in special ways, like when you first began seeing each other. At least once a week, you should go on a "date" (it doesn't count if you take your kids or go along with another couple). The activity needs to be fun—it could be a romantic dinner, a sports event, a trip to the park, or a weekend out of town. This will start the ball rolling to spice up your sex life, even though these activities don't necessarily involve sex.

Next, when you actually get into the bedroom, you should both start spending more time on foreplay. It's easy to hop into bed, have intercourse for a few minutes, and then roll over and go to sleep. But it will be more fun and rewarding to try out some new lingerie or toys, and touch and caress each other before you have sex. Of equal importance is setting the scene for romance, which means that the area should be clean, softly lit by candles or low light, and free of other distractions such as the TV. Massages and baths together are also a great way to get the juices flowing.

Finally, if you just can't think of anything new by yourself, purchase one of the many sex manuals that are on the market, which will tell you in detail how to spark up your sex life. Don't be embarrassed—many couples have a hard time with variety. You might also benefit from buying some sexy clothes. You women should realize that men are naturally very visual and like to look at you in provocative outfits.

And while you men like your women to be knockouts, realize that you should put the same care into your *own* appearance. It's unreasonable to expect that women are going to maintain an attraction if their partners have terrible personal hygiene. So men, understand that women like to feel pretty and don't want to see you in the same pair of dirty underwear night after night.

This takes some effort, but the payoff could be tremendous.

◆ ◆ ◆

Problem #6: "I Have a Headache"

When someone is angry or frustrated in the relationship, it's tempting to withhold sex as a way to punish their partner. It's a way of saying, "If you don't do what *I* want, then I won't do what *you* want." Some couples will go for months or even years without sex because they're playing out other issues from the relationship.

If you start getting the old "I have a headache" excuse, then know that there are sexual problems on the horizon. If you're two healthy adults in a loving relationship, you should *want* to have sex with each other. So, this problem demands a careful analysis and an attempt to find a solution that pleases you both.

Solution #6

It won't help to fight about the last time you had sex because you'll start arguing about whether it was two weeks ago last Friday or three Thursdays ago. Nor does it do any good to pick apart the excuses and invalidate your partner's feelings. Saying things like, "So what if you're stressed? I want some sex!" or "You really aren't that tired!" will only lead to an argument in which you both defend your behavior. You certainly won't get to the root of your problem.

The best approach will be one that seeks to understand the aversion to sex. This means that your initial statement to your partner should be, "Is there something else going on that's causing you to turn off to me?" Let them know that you want to hear the truth and are interested in finding a solution. Avoid the tendency to judge or minimize their feelings, even if you don't agree. (Remember, you're trying to get your sex life back on track, so this is no time to go on the offensive.)

Agree to take your partner's concerns into consideration and make the necessary changes. However, you must also make it clear that withholding sex isn't a coping skill that's going to work in your relationship. You have a right to expect that if there *is* a problem, your partner will verbalize it and not use the tactic of holding your sex life hostage. This is simply unfair to both of you, and it's an immature way to solve problems.

If neither you nor your partner have any desire to have sex again, then it could be a reflection of other more serious personal and psychological issues. As I mentioned earlier, there are medical conditions that can cause a dampening of the sex drive, so you may want to see a health-care professional. It may also be helpful to talk to a counselor and/or sex therapist if things don't improve, since depression and other stressors can dramatically impact normal sexual function.

◆ ◆ ◆

Sex is one of the most enjoyable aspects of a healthy relationship. As I noted earlier, you deserve to experience intimacy and fulfilling sex with your partner. By putting a premium on romance and sex, your relationship can only get better.

■ ■ �◇ O ◇ ■ ■

CHAPTER 7

CHILDREN

In my first book, I stated the following: *A relationship with a shaky foundation will probably not get better with the addition of children.* I then heard from many angry people who accused me of being anti-family and devaluing the importance of children for a couple. Unfortunately, these folks completely missed my point.

Of course, having a family can be an incredibly enriching experience for a couple. However, some people clearly have children for the wrong reasons. Consequently, these kids grow up in broken homes or with parents who resent their existence. Given the high level of child abuse in our society, it's obvious that many kids are being damaged by adults who don't take their parenting seriously. I wish that there was some mandate requiring prospective parents to take a course in raising children, but there isn't— so generations of young people will continue to grow into dysfunctional adults.

If you have a serious relationship problem, I implore you to solve it *before* you make a family addition—you'll do a huge disservice to your kids if you bring them into a relationship that's heading for a breakup or divorce. I understand that many single parents do a wonderful job raising children, but it's certainly not an ideal situation for kids to see their parents fighting and splitting up. So if you think you're responsible enough to *make* a baby, then you better be ready to responsibly care for that child *and* do everything you can to care for your relationship with your partner.

Enough of my lecture. This chapter is about helping you deal with the massive life adjustments that will occur after the birth of your child. Don't be naïve and underestimate the stressors that will rapidly multiply rapidly when you and your partner become parents. I've never spoken to a couple who said that their relationship didn't shift enormously after the birth of a child. Hopefully the changes for you will be positive ones . . . but I'd like to help you negotiate the tough spots that will inevitably arise as you raise a family.

Problem #1: Lack of Family Planning

There are currently unprecedented numbers of unwed mothers and pregnant teens in this country. Children are, by necessity, being raised in single-parent households and by grandparents. This is a problem that can be prevented before it starts, however. And the solution lies in family planning.

I know this is obvious, but I'm going to state it anyway: Every single time you have sex, there's a likelihood that a child could be conceived. Sure, with birth control the odds are greatly reduced, but accidents do happen.

Does this mean that you and your partner should become celibate? Of course not, but you need to be aware that unplanned children can put a huge financial pressure on you; there can be arguments about who's to blame for the pregnancy; you may be resentful and unconsciously take it out on your child; and your relationship may end, putting your child in a tug-of-war between two parents who can't get along. Most of all, it simply isn't fair to bring a child into the world just because you and your partner were too lazy to plan ahead.

Solution #1

I cannot stress enough that you need to *sit down and plan your family with your significant other,* whether you're just dating or you've been married for years. If religious convictions preclude taking any type of birth control, this makes things more difficult but not impossible—you just need to be very disciplined when it comes to planning your sexual activity. If you *can* use birth-control devices, then you both must make the commitment to decide exactly when you want to start a family.

Family planning isn't simply limited to the time frame when a child comes into your lives—you and your partner also need to openly discuss how you'll raise the child. Most couples don't even have this discussion, so they find out too late that there are significant differences in opinion relating to discipline, parental roles, and other forms of involvement with their children. It isn't humanly possible to account for *every* situation that could arise as your child grows up, but it can't hurt to somewhat prepare in advance.

Preventive work in the family-planning area could save your relationship later on and set the foundation for a loving and stable home.

◆ ◆ ◆

Problem #2: The Absentee Parent

This is, sadly, a common problem for couples—one partner is always too busy or involved with other things to become an active participant in their child's life. Children will eventually sense when one parent doesn't care . . . and it doesn't matter if both parents are living at home. I know some divorced parents who are more interested in their children than some married couples are. Maybe I got lucky, because both of my parents supported me and took an active interest in my life as I grew up. *Your* children deserve nothing short of this same degree of attention.

It's your job as a parent to spend time with your kids and do your fair share of the workload. It's irresponsible for you to expect your partner to do everything—you contributed half of the effort to *make* a child, so you should at least do half the work of raising him or her. If you're not willing to do this, then I'd classify you as a "deadbeat," even if you provide financial support. Just making money doesn't get you off the hook, as many people seem to think. Your kids won't fully understand financial matters, but they'll certainly feel abandoned and neglected if you do nothing else for them besides buy them things.

Solution #2

First of all, I give you permission to demand that your partner share in parenting tasks. Unfortunately, you can't force your partner to care for and love your kids, or even to have any contact with them whatsoever. (However, on a separate note, you can and should enforce child support to the fullest extent of the law.)

If you're still married, then you both need to share responsibilities. This translates to an equal division of duties—if you need to delineate actual child-caring chores, so be it. You shouldn't be the one to always get up in the middle of the night, stay at home with your children while your partner goes out, or be the "bad cop" every time your child misbehaves. These are only a few examples, but you get the picture. You and your partner are a team in this endeavor.

If, after confronting your partner about their lack of interest and participation in the parenting experience, there's no change, then it may be time for a serious talk about the state of your relationship in general. Try to appeal to your partner's love for your kids, even if the two of you aren't getting along. If the pattern of neglect continues, you should try to utilize any other means of support you have, including your family and friends. Most likely, someone will step up and help you.

You're then left with an incredibly difficult decision—stay with a partner who ignores his/her family consistently, or raise the kids on your own, perhaps with outside help. I won't lie to you—neither scenario is perfect and will be fraught with its own set of disadvantages. Although I personally don't believe that staying with an absentee partner is doing anyone a favor, including the kids, I can't fault you if you pursue this option—nor would I blame you if you took the other route.

◆ ◆ ◆

Problem #3: Differing Disciplinary Styles

Discipline and limit-setting are perhaps the most important tasks you'll be charged with as parents. How you master this as a couple will go a long way in determining your child's personality and future achievements. This means that you both need to agree on the style and degree of punishments meted out; and more important, realize that the discipline needs to be fair and consistent. But be sure that you have a very good reason to punish your child—don't randomly dole it out just because you've had a bad day.

Here's the way things usually play out for parents: Whatever you received in the way of discipline as a child will tend to be how you choose to treat your kids. It's human nature to do what we've known or experienced, but some of this may be to the detriment of your children. For example, if you were verbally or physically abused as a child, there may be a tendency to repeat the same pattern. At the other extreme, if you were rarely told no as a child or were never given appropriate boundaries, then you may tend to be a hands-off parent who isn't assertive enough. Do you really want to turn into your mom or dad when it comes to discipline?

Solution #3

I'm not going to tell you the exact methods to use in disciplining your kids, but I do feel strongly that striking your children is an unreasonable approach to take. It just doesn't accomplish anything other than making your kids cry and causing them to fear you. Maybe you want to feel powerful and in charge, but does this do your kids any favors? I know that the argument for spanking is strong— a large part of our population swears that children behave better when this type of punishment is used. The problem I have with this is that many people will spank their kids without ever sitting them down to calmly discuss the rules so they can learn from their mistakes. So if you do utilize spanking, I urge you to follow it up with a lesson on appropriate behavior.

Another critical mistake that many couples make is

that they don't agree in advance on a particular penalty, and then the child plays the parents against one another. I always knew that if my mom set up a punishment, my father would be more lenient and take it away. There was a chink in their armor that I was able to exploit—and I don't think that skill particularly helped me throughout my later years.

So you and your significant other need to agree on the exact form of discipline that will be used, as well as what offenses will warrant punishment. Then you must present a united front to your child and *stick with your plan*. It's easy to fall into the trap of revoking a punishment because you begin to feel sorry for your kids. But I believe that if it's a 30-minute timeout, then it should be *30 minutes*. If they're grounded for a week, then it should last a week, not a day or two.

Also, the same bad behavior should deserve the same amount and intensity of discipline each time. What you're both striving for is *consistency* and *agreement*. If these two elements are present, then your kids will know what to expect and learn to think through the consequences of their actions.

◆ ◆ ◆

Problem #4: Trying to Raise the "Perfect Kid"

I've been to countless soccer and Little League games in which the parents seemed to care more about what happened on the field than the kids did. Parents yell and scream at their own children when they make a mistake, which practically ensures that the poor kids will grow up feeling like they're never good enough.

Parents aren't perfect, so it makes no sense to expect kids to be. Children are messy and make mistakes, but most important, they don't think about the world in the same way that adults do. They're going to screw up over and over, and it's a parent's job to accept this and act in a calm and rational fashion.

Consider the following:

- When you were a child, were you expected to act "just right"? If you didn't do so, would your parents level severe punishment against you?

- Are you and your partner just too lazy and selfish to teach your child appropriate behaviors, finding that it's easier to get angry and dish out punishment?

- Do you feel that having a "perfect" child means that you're also "perfect"? In other words, do you see your child as an extension of yourself?

- Is it easier to see faults in someone else who depends on you than it is to focus on your own shortcomings?

- Do you want your extended community (friends, family, neighbors, and so on) to think that you're the greatest parent ever? Do you take pleasure in thinking that your kids are more well behaved than others?

If you answered yes to any of the preceding statements, please read on.

Solution #4

Every time you enroll your kids in another class or activity, or when you become angry because they're not the "best," ask yourself this: *Who am I really doing this for, my children or myself?* I bet you'll find that the gratification is for *you,* and your kids' happiness is secondary.

There's nothing wrong with the desire to see your children succeed in school and activities, but it *is* wrong to constantly berate them if they're not living up to your own set of expectations. When kids are allowed to go at their own pace and make their own choices, there's a natural maturation process that occurs. So one of the most important jobs for you as a parent is to be the support when your kids fall down . . . but you have to let *them* fall down periodically.

Every mistake made by your child should be followed by a lesson aimed at teaching them correct behavior. Yelling or hitting isn't teaching—it's just a process that adds another layer of scars onto a child who doesn't deserve to have a parent who acts like a maniac.

◆ ◆ ◆

Problem #5: A Child with Behavioral Problems

Sometimes, because of genetic illnesses or chemical imbalances, children are unable to control their behavior and emotions, even with understanding and supportive parents who set reasonable limits. These kids need outside assistance, and it's up to you to get it for them.

I'm not talking about kids who occasionally act out and hit their brothers and sisters or who won't clean up their room. Hitting, temper tantrums, and defiance are within the normal realm of childhood behaviors, to a certain degree. The critical thing for you and your partner to gauge is the frequency and intensity of this behavior. I'm not going to kid you—this can be very difficult. You're entering a gray zone when you try to determine the fine line between normal and abnormal behavior.

There are some obvious warning signs that your kids are in trouble, including the following:

- They don't reach developmental milestones and seem to lag behind the curve.

- They engage in self-destructive behavior such as head-banging or intentionally inflicting harm on themselves.

- They're never able to sleep through the night.

- They find it difficult to be away from you for a short period of time (more so than other children and their parents).

- They tear up the house repeatedly (beyond throwing toys around during playtime).

- They hallucinate or are severely depressed and lethargic.

If your kids do exhibit any of these behaviors, then it's time to have them checked out by their pediatrician.

Solution #5

I believe that an integral part of good parenting is your willingness to learn new skills. There are entire sections in bookstores that deal with parenting, and your pediatrician can also provide you with literature and resources that will be of tremendous help.

Most of the resources will agree on one thing, though—if your child has a learning, behavioral, or emotional disorder (which has been properly diagnosed by an expert), your job as the parent becomes that much more important. You'll be giving your child a fighting chance if both you and your partner are able to consistently set firm limits that are explained to your child and then enforced. This is no time for haphazard or inconsistent boundaries, so you and your partner have to function as a team.

You'll need to learn about your child's disorder—treatment, diagnosis, prognosis, and outcomes; and you may, unfortunately, need to consider psychiatric treatment for your child, which may include psychotherapy and/or medication management.

And if you need to enroll your child in a special program or school, please don't think that this is a reflection on you. Know that you're being a better parent by giving your child every possible chance to succeed.

◆ ◆ ◆

I'd like to finish up this chapter by noting a few other very important points. You and your partner will undoubtedly disagree at times about the care of your children. There's nothing wrong with this, unless the children get put into the middle of your own personal and relationship problems. This often happens when parents aren't getting along or are divorced, but no child should be the go-between or the moderator of family conflicts. Whenever you hear yourself say something like "Go tell your daddy (or mommy) that I'm angry about _____," please catch yourself. Children should never negotiate adult relationship problems!

It isn't my goal to school you on child-rearing, but you and your partner absolutely need to do the following for your children:

- Make them feel safe at home. Arguing about your relationship problems in front of them won't accomplish this goal.

- Tell your kids when you've made a mistake when dealing with them.

- Don't blame your children for your marital or relationship issues—and it certainly isn't right to force them to choose one parent over another.

- Let your kids feel secure enough to share things with you, without the threat of excessive criticism.

- Allow your kids to have real childhoods— don't place adult responsibilities on them prematurely.

- Sit down with your partner and decide on a fair set of punishments and rewards that you both agree upon. Your children should always know what to expect when they act in a certain way.

- Most of your kids' life lessons won't be taught in a classroom at school, so *you* two have to be their teachers and role models.

If you make it a point to take a hands-on approach to parenting and make it your number-one goal to set a good example for your children, you'll have the pleasure of raising happy, well-adjusted kids who will become balanced, successful adults.

CHAPTER 8

INFIDELITY

Here's a shocking statistic for you to ponder: Approximately 35 to 40 percent of all married men and 25 percent of all married women cheat on their spouses. Clearly, it's very difficult for a lot of us to honor our vows and commitments to another person for the rest of our lives.

Since it ranks up there as one of the most significant ways to hurt and betray another individual, we're going to take a more in-depth look at infidelity and its associated problems in this chapter. When you find out that your partner has cheated on you, the work is just beginning. Your relationship may survive, but first you need to accept this truth: *Cheating will absolutely change the dynamic of your relationship, and it will never be the same again.* This doesn't mean that there's no chance for redemption—the relationship can continue, but it will have to do so under different rules and guidelines, with an emphasis on trust, and an understanding of what led to the infidelity in the first place.

Problem #1: You Haven't Exactly Defined *Infidelity* for Your Partner

I know that no one wants to think about breaking up as a result of infidelity. It's certainly not a very romantic topic to discuss with your significant other—or maybe you believe that your partner should just intuitively know what's right and what's not. Either way, your expectations may not be in line with your partner's, especially when it comes to interactions with those outside your relationship. That's when the trouble begins.

Solution #1

It's your responsibility to determine what you believe infidelity is and communicate this to your partner. I'll make this easier by offering up my own definition, which was first given to me by Karen Hand, the co-host of my radio show:

Infidelity: You're engaged in a behavior of a sexual or intimate nature that you cannot openly discuss with your partner.

This explanation is perfect, because it covers both the actual act of cheating *and* the subsequent process of concealment and lying. (Notice that it includes nonphysical factors, since you can be intimate with someone without actually touching them.) There shouldn't be any major secrets in your relationship, or the trust and honesty that are necessary elements of a successful union will be missing.

It's now up to you to precisely define what *you* consider to be cheating. Ask yourself the following:

- Can my partner have sexual relations (including, but not limited to, intercourse) with another person?

- Is there a difference between a one-night stand versus an affair? Does the frequency matter, or is it one strike and they're out?

- How much flirting can my significant other engage in with other people?

- How close can my partner get to someone else on a "just friends" basis? Is it okay for them to share personal details about our life together with someone else?

- What is my view on pornography and strip clubs? Can my partner see members of the opposite sex naked, whether "real" or on film or in print?

Your answers to these questions should give you and your partner a jumping-off point for a frank discussion on what constitutes infidelity in your relationship.

◆ ◆ ◆

Problem #2: Your Partner Has Cheated on You

For many people, it's incredibly painful to imagine the most important person in their life having sexual relations with someone else, so they immediately end the relationship without giving their partner a second chance. Yet a larger percentage will choose to stay with someone who's been unfaithful, hoping that things will somehow get better. Many of these people will get cheated on again and again, but some will save the relationship and regain some measure of happiness.

If you do decide to stay together, keep in mind that the relationship will have no chance of surviving if you don't try to accomplish one crucial goal: *Determine exactly why infidelity has become a part of your relationship.* If you and your partner don't seek to understand the behavior and motivation behind the indiscretion, your relationship will have little chance of moving forward. Couples who try to sweep this issue under the rug or assume that it will all just go away are fooling themselves.

Solution #2

Here, I'm going to list the most common reasons behind cheating. Think about whether any of these apply to your own situation. If so, your plan of action should include a no-holds barred discussion about the particular area. (**Note:** I strongly believe that you should have these discussions not only at home, but also with a trained therapist or relationship counselor, since you're probably not going to be able to figure this out on your own. Keep in mind that infidelity is merely a symptom of something else that's drastically wrong with your relationship—it occurs because there are unresolved issues that aren't being addressed. I think that your relationship has little chance of surviving unless you both agree to go to couples' counseling.)

— *Sexual reasons:* This is the area that you two will probably focus on the most, for it's common to feel that your partner cheated on you because your sex life is deficient. I can't deny that there are some people who will cheat simply because of sexual needs; the risk of infidelity is certainly greatly diminished if both partners enjoy having sex with each other.

So ask your partner the following question: "What, if anything, is lacking in our sex life that led you to cheat?" This is difficult, because hearing that things may need to change in this most intimate of areas can be embarrassing. Nevertheless, you *must* talk about it.

— *Emotional reasons:* This could be the area where you and your partner will make the most strides in understanding each other. You'll have to shift your discussions away from sex to an exploration of your emotional states. When cheating occurs, it's natural to think that it must strictly be due to a sexual cause—but many instances of infidelity actually take place as a result of emotional needs. The third party may be providing some kind of support that isn't present in the main relationship, or the cheater may be seeking an emotional escape from their home life—they can have sex and leave the third party, no strings attached.

People also cheat because they feel anger and resentment toward their partner. It becomes difficult to verbalize these feelings within the context of the relationship, so the cheater performs an act designed to hurt their significant other. Some cheaters don't even care if they're caught; in fact, on a subconscious level, they actually hope that they *will* be.

Also look at the issue of boredom. Relationships can lose their spark after a number of years, but instead of communicating this to their partner, the cheater goes outside the relationship to try to create some excitement.

— *You never took a stand:* You may not want to hear this, but the truth is that *you* may need to share some of the blame for your partner's indiscretions. I'm not talking about the first time you find out that your partner has betrayed you—this may come out of the blue, and it isn't your fault. However, after you find out that your partner has cheated on you, you need to take decisive steps to stop the behavior. Don't live in a fantasy world where your partner will just magically see the light and never cheat again—most research indicates that if you take a cheater back without any help or therapy, they'll cheat on you again. Yet if you make it crystal clear that infidelity will not be tolerated but *will* be met with the end of the relationship, your partner will probably think twice before having sexual relations with someone else.

— *There's baggage from the past:* Did your partner's parents cheat on each other or keep secrets? Was your partner lied to or betrayed by significant others from the past? Is there a pattern of cheating on other love interests?

I'm always amazed when someone who's fooling around with a married man or woman believes that *they* won't be cheated on in the future. A friend of mine was the mistress of a married man, and then they ended up in a relationship together. She was devastated when he proceeded to cheat on her with someone else. It seemed like a no-brainer to me—why would she think that somehow she could keep him from cheating? After all, she knew firsthand that he was capable of infidelity because she'd been his mistress!

Your job here is relatively easy: Ask questions and keep your eyes open. Even if you have to ask your partner's friends and associates for information on their past experiences, do so before it's too late.

◆ ◆ ◆

Problem #3: You Missed the Signs

It may be that you're the "last one to know," or you're simply denying that your loved one could be with someone else and hurt you tremendously. Now, I don't want you to walk around feeling paranoid and suspicious for no reason—but if you suspect that something's up, you may be right.

Solution #3

Learn to detect the red flags of infidelity:

- Your partner begins to spend a lot of time away from home, either "working late" or going out with "friends." Maybe there *is* a lot of work to do, but be aware that this may be a sign that trouble is brewing.

- Your partner is evasive about details of daily activities. If there's nothing to hide, then there won't be any hesitation to answer your innocent questions. If you hear, "It's none of your business!" then you need to be on guard.

- You find unfamiliar addresses or telephone numbers. I'm not telling you to rifle through your partner's purse or wallet, but if you happen to find suspicious-looking scraps of paper or business cards, you need to take this as a sign of possible behind-the-scenes activity. It's perfectly acceptable to ask, "I was just wondering—who is that?" Again, an angry, defensive, or defiant response should be a tip-off.

- There's a dramatic change in your partner's appearance or behavior. Is there a shift in your sex life, especially a dwindling of sexual contact? If you and your partner don't have sex anymore, it's fair to wonder if someone else has entered the picture. If your partner starts to take an unusual interest in their physical appearance (buying a new wardrobe or exercising), it may be the case that an effort is being made to impress someone else.

If any of these red flags are present in your relationship, you need to confront your partner about your concerns immediately, and stress to him or her what constitutes cheating in your book.

♦ ♦ ♦

Problem #4: Your Partner Doesn't Want to Save Your Relationship

When infidelity has occurred, two things must happen if there's to be any chance of salvaging the relationship.

First, the cheater must be willing to give up the affair. Second, they must agree to do *whatever it takes* to make your relationship whole again—be it couples' counseling, a renewal of the marriage vows, or a trial separation.

Solution #4

This one is really straightforward—if your partner won't agree to the above conditions, then you should take action to end the relationship now. This is the most caring thing you can do for yourself. There's no other option, unless you're masochistic and desire a lot more pain in the future.

In addition, your partner must let you be angry and gradually learn to trust again. They must be patient—after all, they lost their right to tell you how to feel when they broke the covenant to stay true to you. It won't help you to punish your partner for the rest of your lives, but it's okay to take some time to regain trust. However, if you find that you can never regain faith in your partner, no matter how hard you try or how much time has passed, then read on.

♦ ♦ ♦

Problem #5: You Can Never Trust Your Partner Again

I won't fault you if you simply can't feel the same level of love and trust for your unfaithful partner again. You may have trouble with the image of them having sex with someone else, or the details of the affair may be so incredibly hurtful that you just want your partner to go away forever. This is understandable.

The question is whether you can *ever* attain the same

level of trust that was present before the infidelity. Some couples work through it and go on to a healthy and loving relationship; others find that the cheating tears everything apart to the point that they can never go back.

Solution #5

You shouldn't have to live your life with someone you have little confidence in. At the end of the day, you'll be miserable. So you need to ask yourself these two questions:

1. *Am I still in love with my partner?* If the answer to this question is no, then it's time to admit that you need to move in a different direction. I know that love is a nebulous emotion, but why stay with someone just to prove a point? It's not as if any of your friends or family members will think that you're being strong if you've got nothing left emotionally.

2. *Is there any happiness left for us?* It may be that the pain and humiliation outweighs any sense of joy between you. You might still feel some degree of love for your partner, but your relationship ceases to be fun, or maybe the infidelity is just the final straw in a relationship that went bad long ago. If this is the case, why stay with someone and muddle along? You deserve the chance to find someone else who will love you unconditionally and honestly.

♦ ♦ ♦

I know this is a very difficult and painful subject to deal with, but with time, support, and a lot of work, you *will* make it through . . . and your relationship just might, too.

CHAPTER 9

THE DIFFICULT PARTNER

If you look at the relationship pyramid on page xiv, you'll see that the top of the pyramid contains this statement: *Make your partner feel good about themselves each day.* This can be difficult, since everybody gets caught up in the activities of daily living. But this chapter deals with specific behavior that violates the two rules that define a great relationship:

1.   Your partner's number one-goal should be to treat you with respect and dignity *at all times.*

2.   There must be a spirit of teamwork—you should always work through problems in a cooperative way, and compromise should be effected without fear of future retribution.

The intent of this chapter is to define those behaviors that your partner engages in on a continual basis that may irreversibly harm your relationship and self-esteem. So please read this information carefully.

Problem #1: You Can Never Please Your Partner

You should be praised for the things you do to enhance your relationship. Maybe you won't get a formal thank-you note, but you ought to receive *some* acknowledgment once in a while. After all, relationships thrive in an atmosphere of mutual contentment and positive feedback. If you're with a partner who constantly criticizes (or never recognizes) your strong points, serious trouble could lie ahead.

Solution #1

I've treated adults who never felt they were good enough at anything they did because during the childhood years their parents ignored their accomplishments. They always felt "less than" and insecure, and were destined to perpetuate these feelings in their future relationships.

However, if someone is simply asking for a reasonable amount of recognition and is met with an abusive or unresponsive partner, then *that's* the person with the problem. At that point, action must be taken in an attempt to communicate feelings and take the necessary steps toward one's relationship goals.

— *Step 1:* Try to figure out why it's so difficult for your partner to be a giving person. Even though it's natural for people to be kind and generous to one another, some of us simply won't allow our-selves to act this way. If this applies to your partner, keep in mind that the second you call them on their behavior, their first reaction may be one of defensiveness and denial. They might say, "Hey, I gave you a compliment a few weeks ago—I told you that you looked nice!" This could then lead into a "he said, she said" argument where you go back and forth on how many times you were acknowledged. But don't give up. Make your partner understand that it's really important for you to feel good about yourself when the two of you interact. And resist the temptation to make a list of "slights"—if things digress into how many compliments are offered versus how many criticisms, nothing will ever get resolved. It's more productive to explore why it's so difficult for your partner to open up in a loving way.

— *Step 2:* Call attention to the positive by praising your partner whenever they do something that helps you or the relationship. This may seem pretty generous, especially if you're getting nothing in return. I predict, however, that over time, your partner will come around and join in— it will be a mutual lovefest of sorts. If they don't, it's time for the next step.

— *Step 3:* Decide when enough is enough. How long will you stay with someone who's surly, mean-spirited, and condescending? This is your call—no one else can decide for you. But keep in mind that if you decide to leave this relationship, you'll then be free to find someone who *will* value you and will tell you so. You just need to make a supreme effort to overcome the little voice inside that says: "You're not good enough for anyone to love."

♦ ♦ ♦

Problem #2: Your Partner Publicly Humiliates You

Many of us know a couple who can't get along to save their lives and who pick at each other constantly. I once went to a dinner party and watched a husband berate his wife in front of everyone—he criticized her dress, makeup, hair, and conversation skills. Anytime she spoke up, he'd cut her off with: "God, you're so stupid! You don't know what you're talking about!" She eventually started to sob and left the room. His offhand response was, "She'll get over it."

Of course there are times when your partner may occasionally say or do something that embarrasses you, but it will turn into a major conflict if they insist on ridiculing you in public so that others can witness your pain. This is sadistic and actually a reflection of your partner's own insecurities.

Solution #2

First of all, you need to believe that you deserve to be treated well by your partner. This means that you've got to ignore that voice in your head that says you're not good enough, smart enough, funny enough, or attractive enough. (My father always reminded me that there are enough people in the world who won't hesitate to treat me badly if given the chance, so why should I treat myself badly first?)

Then, you must *in no uncertain terms* tell your verbally abusive partner that you will not tolerate this behavior any longer. I personally believe that if your partner refuses to stop, then it's a relationship-ender. Your problems should be dealt with in private, so do yourself a big favor and demand respect. If you don't get it, find someone who *will* treat you the way you deserve.

♦ ♦ ♦

Problem #3: Your Partner Puts Others First

When you enter into a committed relationship, it's not unreasonable to assume that *you* are now number one in your partner's book and should be treated accordingly. Your partner may maintain that their parents, friends, or career should be on par with you—yet I guarantee that you'll begin to feel resentment and envy if you're relegated to a supporting role.

I received a call on my radio show recently from a man whose wife still spent a lot of time with her ex-husband. In fact, she actually spent more time with him and his family than she did with her current spouse! This man felt awful about it, but he thought if he asked his wife for equal treatment, he'd appear greedy and childish. I helped him realize that his wife needed to commit time to *him* first and others second.

If your partner doesn't want to spend any quality time with you or always makes excuses to be away from home, you need to take immediate action.

Solution #3

As I mentioned, you have every right to be the most important person in the world to your partner. This doesn't mean that other people should be shunned, but they definitely need to come second to *you*.

This solution means that your partner will do the following:

1. Consult with you *before* making plans with others.

2. Include you in family functions and not automatically take their family's side in conflicts.

3. Spend more time with you than any other person in the world.

♦ ♦ ♦

Problem #4: Your Partner Refuses to Get Help

Serious relationship problems require a concerted attempt by both of you to find a solution or middle ground—and you may need professional help to do so. Yet some people won't acknowledge the severity of a problem, which is incredibly arrogant and naïve. Some conflicts, unless tackled with the help of a counselor or therapist, will lead to the destruction of your relationship. You shouldn't be talked into believing that your problems will either (a) magically go away, or (b) be easily solved by the two of you if there's a chronic failure to do so.

You need to be with someone who will at least try to seriously analyze your problems. If you're with a partner who's just too lazy, proud, or stubborn to admit that things aren't right, then you'll be fighting your battles alone.

Solution #4

You can't force someone to attend a counseling session or to fully participate if they do go. Take this into consideration—why would you want to stay with someone who has no interest in saving your relationship? If, however, your partner agrees to get some help, then you've both taken a step in the right direction, and there's hope for you two as a couple.

◆ ◆ ◆

No matter what your partner decides, I encourage you to educate yourself about relationship dynamics—this includes reading self-help materials, attending seminars, and going to a therapist by yourself. You may still find that you'll be able to sort out your feelings so you can make an informed and rational decision about the viability of your relationship. In the process, you just might acquire better coping skills and enhanced self-esteem. This, in and of itself, is a great gift to give yourself.

CHAPTER 10

BLIND DEVOTION

Some partners just bring out the worst in you—but even as you destroy each other's lives in an endless cycle of arguments, emotional abuse, physical altercations, and other relationship problems, you just can't seem to let go. It's as if a magnet has drawn you together, blinding you to the reality that you're just not compatible. I call this phenomenon "blind devotion."

Problem #1: No One Knows Your Partner Like You Do

If you ever hear yourself expressing this sentiment, a big red flag should go up immediately. You'll usually find yourself making this statement after someone has pointed out the problems in your relationship. Your defenses go up, and you retaliate by effectively shutting down the conversation. After all, who can really argue this point with you?

Of course you know personal things about your partner that no one else does . . . but you may also be ignoring some more obvious signals that others are picking up on.

Most people will eventually leave a relationship if it's bad most of the time. However, if your partner is disrespectful sporadically yet has moments of tenderness and generosity, it will be natural to feel confused, especially when you factor in what others are saying. So what should you do?

Solution #1

First, objectively analyze your partner's strengths and weaknesses. This may be tough to do, but be honest—are abuse, abandonment, disrespect, and infidelity *ever* good for a relationship?

Next, if most of the people who care about you are imploring you to leave your partner, you may want to listen. Not all of them can be wrong—yet I've heard many people in similar situations insist that other people "don't know what they're talking about!" Maybe *you're* the one who can't see the forest for the trees, and you should give your loved ones some credit for noticing things that you can't.

♦ ♦ ♦

Problem #2: Your Partner Is a Loser

My definition of a "loser" may be quite different from yours, but I think that we can agree on some basic characteristics.

For example, you may be with someone who has no desire whatsoever to make a good home for you, to devote time and energy to your family and children, to stay consistently employed, or to treat you and others with respect. Perhaps your partner cheats, lies, or does hurtful things behind your back . . . no matter, the result is the same—you're forced to become the responsible one in the relationship, while your partner is the lazy or irresponsible (or even law-breaking) one.

Why would you stay with someone like this? Ask yourself the following questions:

- Do I maintain the false hope that my partner will finally "see the light" and get their act together, even if there's no evidence to the contrary?

- Do I feel that since we vowed to stay together for "better or worse," I just need to put up with this behavior?

- Do I realize on some level that I made a poor decision about my partner, yet I'm too proud to admit that I made a mistake?

If you answered yes to any of these questions, you're blindly devoted to a loser who's going to take you right down with them.

Solution #2

Honestly examine your relationship. Know that if your partner really, truly cared about you, they would have made every attempt to stay out of trouble and lead a responsible life. I simply don't see how someone could claim to love you while they're continually drinking, drugging, cheating, not working, breaking laws, or abusing you or the family. It just doesn't add up.

What can you do? You've got two choices:

1. Do nothing; and lead a life filled with uncertainty, insecurity, and anxiety.

2. Demand that your partner take responsibility for their actions so that they do whatever's best for you and your family *at all times.*

Which will it be for you? Remember that others will ultimately classify you in the same way as those with whom you closely associate. Therefore, it will be impossible for you to say, "Well, I may be with a loser, but *I'm* not one." Yes, you are—after all, you're the one who made the choice to be with this person.

◆ ◆ ◆

Problem #3: You're Addicted to Making Up

You had a horrible fight with your partner, and you feel awful. However, the next day you get a bouquet of flowers, a new piece of jewelry, or plane tickets to a romantic locale. Suddenly if feels like it did when you first started dating. This all sounds pretty good, right? I mean, who doesn't want to be swept off their feet? The problem is that this behavior doesn't come from a genuine place—it's a thinly veiled attempt by your partner to win you over after they did something wrong. The cycle is this:

Partner treats you badly——▶ an argument
ensues——▶ the relationship is in danger——▶
your partner apologizes for the behavior and
showers you with affection and/or gifts in order

to keep you in the relationship —→ you're then overwhelmed and eager to lap up any morsel of love —→ relationship continues.

You may be addicted to the euphoric feelings associated with making up, since it's the only positive attention you get from your partner. Yet this blinds you to the reality that your partner must have done something very wrong to lead to this whole situation in the first place. It's almost as if the process of breaking up and making up has taken on an aphrodisiacal quality. In my first book, I called this the "relationship roller coaster," where the ups and down of the "ride" can be so exhilarating that you forget there's an option to get off.

Solution #3

You need to accept the fact that making up over and over isn't going to sustain your relationship. What happens before your partner asks for another chance? They've made a mistake (sometimes a big one), and they want you to be distracted by their subsequent wooing. This doesn't do a thing to address the root of your problems.

It's time to stop your devotion to make-up situations. Instead, you and your partner should make a concerted effort to discuss potential problems *before* things get out of hand. And you should insist that your partner show you love and respect even when nothing's wrong!

Fight the urge to stay on a relationship roller coaster, for your relationship won't be able to sustain its highs and lows. A boring relationship isn't the answer, but a *predictable* one will stand the test of time.

♦ ♦ ♦

Problem #4: You Chose a Partner Out of Spite

Rebellious teenagers sometimes date people their parents hate just to make waves and shake things up a bit. This is a common adolescent coping skill, which helps them start the process of separating from their parents and declaring their own independence.

Since I assume that you're no longer a teenager, you shouldn't be employing this tactic any longer. Yet you may be tempted to date a "bad boy (or girl)" as a convenient way to proclaim, "I'll do what I want, and you can't stop me!" Not only is this an angry gesture, it's also completely unfair to the person you're with, who's being used to generate controversy. So grow up and be with a partner for the *right* reasons—that is, you have fun together, share common interests, are physically attracted to one another, and genuinely like each other.

Solution #4

If you continue to see someone whom your family or friends dislike, think about the real reasons behind your behavior. Do your loved ones wish to see you fail? Or are you angry with them for not supporting your choice? If the latter is the case, ask yourself if it's worth sacrificing happiness because you're upset with other people. I mean, do you want to live as a spiteful, revenge-seeking person who only hurts yourself (and your partner) in the end? You can certainly assert your power and independence in many positive ways, instead of by trying to shock everyone by making a poor relationship decision.

♦ ♦ ♦

Keep in mind that if you're blindly devoted to someone who's no good for you, it's probably best to listen to
the opinions of the people you trust. Know that they
really just want you to be happy. And even if you do feel
a magnetic pull toward this person, remember that *truly
wise people know when to cut their losses and move on.*

CHAPTER 11

JEALOUSY
AND CONTROL

Jealousy is an incredibly complex emotion caused by the fear of losing someone or something to a rival. And it's so common that if I had to pick one motivating force behind wars, crime, violence, and greed, jealousy would certainly top the list.

But notice that I also included the word *control* in the title of this chapter. That's because a jealous person will almost always attempt to control the actions and emotions of their partner, for if someone is controlled, they'll hypothetically be less likely to abandon their significant other. Therefore, by being in charge and making the rules, the jealous partner feels more secure. And so:

> Insecurity and low self-esteem—►leads to the emotion of jealousy—►leads to controlling behavior.

So we can see that a partner who tries to control is really experiencing internal turmoil, which is a symptom of an underlying insecurity. Now they can be seen in a different light—as someone who lacks confidence and feels unsure about their own ability to secure someone's love. Therefore, the controlling partner is really showing a "false self" to the world in an attempt to cover up their own fears and anxieties.

I think that the answer to dealing with a consistently jealous and controlling partner is quite simple—get out of the relationship! But this isn't necessarily easy to accomplish, especially when you're afraid that your partner will do whatever they can to force you to stay with them. Remember, their fear of losing you will fuel the jealousy, so it's natural for them to up the ante when you realize that you've had enough and want to leave. They may even threaten retribution, physical violence, stalking, or suicide, but this craziness should only convince you even more that you need to extricate yourself from the relationship.

There are a number of problems associated with jealousy and control, so let's just examine the most serious ones.

Problem #1: Your Nice, Rational
Partner Suddenly Turns into a Raving Lunatic

In the beginning, your partner swept you off your feet. As you were wined and dined and lavished with gifts and attention, you felt as if you were in a dream. Everything was going beautifully, and you fell in love. But then, the tone changed dramatically. Instead of wanting to *see* you every day, this person wanted to *keep track of you* every day. You were encouraged to stop seeing your friends and family. The flowers stopped arriving, and the romance dried up. Despite your hopes and prayers, things never went back to the way they were, and you found that you were stuck with a jealous, controlling partner.

At that point it may have seemed impossible to leave the relationship because the more you were controlled and pushed around, the more you felt threatened and insecure. But freedom *can* be a reality. Read on.

Solution #1

First, ask yourself the following question: "Am I doing anything to warrant this jealousy?" If you *are*—for example, you're staying out all night, cheating, acting suspiciously, or excluding your partner from parts of your life— then the jealousy may be a reasonable response to your behavior.

But if you aren't doing anything to cause your partner to become jealous and controlling, then you have to take action to address the situation *immediately*. You must sit down with your partner and tell them the following: "I cannot be with a jealous and controlling person. I know that you think that acting this way will make it less likely for me to leave you. But the opposite is going to happen—this behavior will push me away even quicker. If you continue to act this way, I can't be with you. You need to back off and let me be who I am."

They'll probably say that they just want you to be happy; they may even try to get you to admit that you're considering ending the relationship (making them justified in their jealousy). Don't fall for this manipulation. The longer you allow your partner to be the dominant force, the harder it will be to change the pattern.

If you can't do what I've suggested, then consider the following: Jealousy usually doesn't get better by itself—in fact, things usually get worse, progressing to much more punitive methods of control, including verbal and physical abuse.

Also keep in mind that a partner who comes on really strong early in the relationship (and wants to be with you every waking moment) may be the type to exhibit intense jealousy and control later on. Just because someone seems like a prince at first doesn't necessarily mean that they won't turn back into a frog as the relationship progresses.

◆ ◆ ◆

Problem #2: Your Partner Tries to Isolate You from Others

The movie *Sleeping with the Enemy,* starring Julia Roberts and Patrick Bergin, shows in graphic detail what can happen if you become isolated and totally dependent on a controlling partner. If you've never seen it, here's a synopsis: Julia and Patrick's characters are married and live in a remote beach house. She has no friends, family members, or close associates nearby, as he's gotten her to believe that she needs to get away from all of her old people and "start fresh" with him. He does the shopping and goes to work while she sits isolated and helpless in their home.

As soon as he returns each day, he checks the house thoroughly to make sure that she's had no visitors. He also demands that she act "perfectly" for him—that is, he measures how straight the towels are hung or how tidy the cupboards are. Anything out of step incites him to beat her. The cycle of physical abuse continues to the point that she fakes her own death to start a new life in another town a thousand miles away. (Since this is a Hollywood movie, the husband hunts her down, thus setting the stage for an explosive and violent ending.)

I certainly hope that your relationship doesn't turn out like this, but the point I'm trying to make is that you need to stay in touch with your friends and family even if you're in a dream relationship. Isolation could make you dependent on a jealous and controlling significant other, which is a terrible position to be in.

Solution #2

You must do two things to avoid this relationship problem:

1. Make every attempt to keep in touch with your loved ones. It's downright rude to ignore your friends and family members just because you're flying high. What happens if you crash? Will you have done so much damage to your connection with them that you have no one to turn to during the rough times? Plus, it's never good to relate to just one other person—you need some variety in your life.

2. If your partner tells you to drop your friends and family, know that this is extremely selfish and disrespectful. It's also a warning sign that your partner is highly insecure and jealous, which could get out of hand as the relationship progresses. You're nobody's possession, so you shouldn't be told whom to associate with. Adamantly resist your partner's wish to isolate you from the world—don't let them wield that much power over you.

♦ ♦ ♦

Problem #3: Your Partner
Wants to Make All the Decisions

The best relationships are "run" by *both* partners. For example, some nights my wife decides what to have for dinner, while other nights I make the call. We share the responsibility equally—because we're both mature enough to let the other have their way. This is a simple example, but it illustrates our ability to share. No matter whether the decision is large or small, we both have input.

The jealous and controlling partner won't allow you to have any ideas of your own. The jealous part of them can't admit that maybe you're smart, too; and the controlling part of them feels the need to make all the decisions. It may be easy for you to sit back and go with the flow, but trust me, this tendency will ultimately make your life much more difficult. You'll have absolutely no say in anything that happens in your relationship, and you'll eventually feel smothered.

You mustn't allow yourself to get into this situation. Here's the solution.

Solution #3

Early on in your relationship, you need to develop a presence as a decisive person and offer up your input regarding any major decision that affects you both. Whether your partner agrees with you or not isn't the point—but you'll have sent the message that you're assertive and you won't be arbitrarily controlled and pushed around. Then you can both compromise and decide together what path seems best.

If your partner insists that all decisions must go their way, then know that you've committed to a selfish narcissist who's on a power trip at your expense. Over time you'll grow very unhappy unless you have the courage to make the one decision that's yours and yours alone—to end the relationship and find a more amenable partner.

♦ ♦ ♦

Problem #4: Your Partner Can't Be Proud of You

Your jealous partner just can't say, "Good job! I'm really proud of you." Instead, they secretly wish you to fail because this will prove that they're indeed brighter and more talented than you are. And if you try something new and don't succeed, your jealous partner will either pepper you with insulting or degrading remarks or won't say anything at all.

Perhaps your partner had an undemonstrative parent who never showed them any love. If that's the case, they should get help—it's not fair for you to be the recipient of their childhood baggage. But regardless of what the motivation is, when jealousy enters your relationship, it becomes a race to see who's "better" . . . a race nobody can win.

Solution #4

There's no way to force your partner to be supportive or to say nice things to you. No matter how perfect you are or how much you accomplish, your partner may never be able to provide the acceptance you long for.

However, it's reasonable for you to need some sort of emotional support. If your partner is willing (which I doubt they will be), explore why it's difficult for them to say kind words to you. Then, if the pattern doesn't change for the better, you have to decide to do things just for yourself. You may be surprised to learn that your partner is left in your wake as you expand your circle of friends and bring some excitement into your life.

♦ ♦ ♦

As you deal with a jealous partner, just remember that a person who really loves you will be on your side and root for you to succeed in life. Even if you fall flat on your face, they'll be there to pick you up and offer words of encouragement and support because they value you. They'll want you to be your own person, pick your friends, dress how you want, and have the freedom to pursue your own interests and dreams. A truly loving mate allows you to keep growing as a person, rather than attempting to mold you into what they want. So control your own destiny—don't let another person's jealous and controlling nature stand in your way.

■ ■ ◇ O ◇ ■ ■

CHAPTER 12

ANGER

Can you remember a time when you were extremely angry at your significant other? How did you express yourself—did you yell and scream, throw things, or just slink away and pout for days?

If you grew up in a home where anger wasn't managed correctly and matters got out of hand, then you probably think of it as a destructive emotion. Whether your parents had knock-down, drag-out fights or didn't speak to each other for days—the message was sent that anger causes people to act irrationally and even ruin their relationships.

If you were really lucky, your childhood experience was different, and you were able to see your parents come together to calmly and rationally discuss their relationship conflicts. Your mom and dad may have been upset with each other, but they dealt with their problems and moved on. And so, as you got older, you learned to channel angry feelings constructively.

I hope that after you've read this chapter, you'll actually be able to use anger to your advantage and develop effective techniques for managing any frustrations you might have. In fact, I don't think that you have much choice in this matter—if you refuse to learn how to control your anger or if you stay with someone who's full of rage, then this decision will impact your life in very negative ways. So it's time to leave behind the yelling and silent treatments and choose peace and tranquility.

Problem #1: Your Partner Randomly Directs Their Anger at You

Many children grow up being the target of their parents' anger, for no discernible reason other than they were there. Kids who were raised in this kind of an environment often grow up to do the same thing to *their* significant others. If your partner falls into this category, the balance of power in your relationship is one-sided. Here's why:

> Random anger is used as a psychological weapon to gain the upper hand—➤ your angry partner gets the power of surprise, which keeps you off balance—➤ your power is diminished since you're constantly on the defensive.

Keep this in mind: *A partner who is consistently or randomly angry has psychological issues that have absolutely nothing to do with you.* Yet how can you be expected to live happily in an environment where, no matter how hard you try, anger constantly comes your way?

Solution #1

I'll first tell you what *not* to do if your partner yells at you for no reason: *Don't just take it!* This doesn't mean that you need to yell back and engage in a nasty conflict; instead, emphatically tell your partner that you're not in the relationship to get treated like a child. And also tell them that there must be a solid basis for their rage (in other words, they can't just be having a bad day) or you simply won't be able to listen to the complaint.

This approach may work, and your partner just might back down and treat you with respect. However, you may be with someone who's just mean-spirited and angry all the time. For example, a former patient of mine kept telling me that his wife constantly yelled at him. At first I found this hard to believe, but when I saw them together, it turned out to be true. No matter how calm he stayed, she'd let loose with a fiery rage that just wouldn't subside. Even *I* couldn't derail her fury—she had no insight whatsoever into the real source of her anger and didn't seem particularly interested in determining what caused it. My patient called her "a living nightmare," and after seeing her in action, I had to agree. He decided to leave her, which wasn't easy—but he was finally a free man.

If you have a partner like this man's wife, you might have to make a tough decision to leave the person whom you love but can't live with on a daily basis. After all, walking on eggshells is no way to go through life.

♦ ♦ ♦

Problem #2: Your Partner Can't Take Criticism

At times you may have to offer constructive criticism to your partner. There's nothing wrong with saying something like, "I really want us to talk about your habit of doing _____, which is really beginning to impact our relationship."

Reasonable people will be open to discussion, but you might find that you're met with an angry and defiant partner who can't tolerate even the slightest bit of criticism, no matter how nicely it's phrased. For example, if you ask your husband to stop watching TV long enough to go to lunch together, and he reacts by ignoring you and turning the TV up louder, then you've got a bigger problem than just neglect—you now have to deal with an angry, passive-aggressive spouse.

Emotions rarely help the problem-solving process. If your partner reacts by throwing a temper tantrum, then no progress will be made. Adults rationally consider a piece of criticism and calmly respond, while children take it personally and react quite emotionally. So think about it: Are you involved in a relationship with a child in an adult's body?

Solution #2

Once your partner has lost control in an emotional fashion, little can be accomplished at that particular moment. Engaging in a shouting match will do nothing to make the situation better, and walking away without acknowledging their anger can exacerbate the tension even more. But there *is* a middle ground that you can reach. The following phrase will defuse the immediate situation and still leave the door open for future discussion: "I can't continue to talk to you until we can deal with this problem in a calm manner. We just won't get anything accomplished when you're like this. Let's agree to take some time off from this subject and try again later."

This sounds like a lot to say, but it could be incredibly

helpful for you both. It gives your partner permission to cool down, and allows you to escape from an angry tirade. Hopefully the problem can be tackled at a later time, and the outcome will be more productive.

If there's no way to have a reasonable and calm conversation at any time, then you need to ask yourself why you're with someone who can't seem to control their anger.

♦ ♦ ♦

Problem #3: Your Partner Blows Up at Other People

Here's an old saying that you should give some consideration to: "Look at the way your partner treats other people around you [family, friends, strangers, and so on], for this is the way you'll eventually be treated." I absolutely believe in this statement, because I've seen it played out time and time again.

A friend of mine once dated a man who treated her like a goddess in private—but in public, he was rude and demeaning to anyone he came in contact with—from people in service positions to his co-workers, friends, and family members. It was as if she were dating two totally different guys . . . but he was nice to *her*, so she continued on in the relationship and made excuses for this man's bad behavior. Unfortunately, as time went by, she started to get hints that his public displays were indicative of his real personality—until she finally became the target of his anger as well.

Sure, it's easy to get sucked into the charms of someone who makes you feel "special" and different, and it's also tempting to enter into a love relationship in which it's "the two of us against the world"—but if your partner is rude and initiates conflicts with others, they'll do the very same thing to you. It may not happen today, but it *will* happen.

Solution #3

You can't afford to be oblivious to the effect your partner has on other people: If they treat others poorly, then be warned that you'll probably be the recipient of the same treatment down the road.

Moreover, do you want to be thought of as someone who stays with a complete jerk? This is a big-time reflection on your own character, and in the process of defending this type of partner, you may also lose other valuable relationships.

You could encourage your rude partner to seek out ways to manage anger (through therapy, perhaps), but you need to put your foot down and demand that they clean up their act in the meantime.

◆ ◆ ◆

Problem #4: Your Partner Gives You the Silent Treatment

Some people have the tendency to show their displeasure and anger by withdrawing their love and communication—a passive-aggressive tactic that's infuriating to the person on the receiving end. Silence only serves to heighten tension and compound a problem, as the couple plays a waiting game to see who will crack first.

Why would your partner refuse to discuss a problem that needs to be solved? There are actually a few possible reasons:

- They don't want to risk losing an argument, so they shut down the debate.

- They saw their parents use this coping skill, so they're just doing what they know.

- It's a way to punish you when they think you're getting in their way. You then feel guilty and on edge because you upset them.

- They secretly hope that if they're quiet long enough, the problem will disappear.

- They're ultimately scared to death to express anger, which they believe is unacceptable. So the next best thing is to withdraw in silence.

The silent treatment can be devastating to your relationship . . . so what can you do when you feel like you're talking to a brick wall?

Solution #4

Try to communicate to your partner that silence won't make your problems go away. Tell them that you want an active dialogue—offer to just listen to their side of things without interruption and judgment, and tell them that you'll do your best to compromise and do whatever is necessary to come up with a solution.

If your partner is firmly entrenched in their silence, then there's really not much you can do, except to decide when you've had it. It's fair to warn them that their habit of giving you the silent treatment is ultimately going to make you reevaluate your relationship. Ultimately, you need to be with someone who will work *with* you to manage disagreements.

♦ ♦ ♦

Suffice it to say that anger is a scary emotion for most of us—we often get irrational and do things we later regret. Therefore, it isn't surprising that most people will do just about anything to avoid a confrontation with their partner. Yet anger can actually be quite constructive, *if* it's tempered and contained. Unrestrained anger is dangerous, because there's no purpose in mind and no end result to achieve. Think about this for a moment: You and your partner will lose a part of yourselves each time there's a situation that regresses into an insult-calling match.

I won't kid you—there's no perfect solution to dealing with an angry partner. Your ultimate options are:

1. Make an unbreakable agreement that only positive language will be used toward each other.

2. Continue on the destructive path of vindictiveness, which will destroy your psyche.

3. Consider ending the relationship to reclaim your sense of dignity.

The real danger associated with anger is discussed in the next chapter—that is, when it leads to physical and/or emotional abuse. I wish that I didn't have to write about this topic, but you need to know the facts. They just may save your life.

■ ■ ◇ O ◇ ■ ■

CHAPTER 13

EMOTIONAL AND PHYSICAL ABUSE

A lthough it seems unbelievable, millions of people stay with verbally and/or physically abusive partners. I've personally counseled countless victims of domestic abuse who were admitted into the emergency room, beaten to within an inch of their lives . . . only to go home with their abuser for another round.

This subject deeply saddens me, so in this chapter, I'll try to make sense of why people stay with abusive partners. You'll notice that the format here is different from other chapters. That's because I really have only one solution for each one of these scenarios: *Do whatever you can to end the relationship <u>right now.</u>* It's the only thing that makes sense for you and your kids (if you have them).

But first let's find out why you'd want to stay with a partner who calls you names, ridicules your efforts, humiliates you in front of others, and inflicts bodily harm.

Reason #1: On Some Level,
You Honestly Feel As If You Deserve the Abuse

When I've asked abused people why they put up with such treatment, one of the most common answers I've heard is, "I guess I had it coming. I made a mistake, and I deserved it." Many victims of abuse have experienced similar treatment in the past, either during childhood or in previous relationships—in other words, they've been programmed to believe that they're somehow "bad" and need to be punished.

This is an incredibly difficult thought process to change. Usually these feelings have been imprinted on the victim's brain for many years and can often only be remedied by psychotherapy.

If you find yourself in this category, I urge you to seek professional help. You need to generate positive feelings about yourself, which may help you break free of an abusive cycle.

Reason #2: You're Afraid to Be Alone

Many people feel like total losers unless they're in a relationship—to them, being alone is frightening and sends the message that they're not desirable. Consequently, these people will do anything to have *any* relationship, even if it means that they get an angry and abusive partner in the process.

If this is your pattern, ask yourself what's worse—staying connected to a person who calls you names, degrades you, or strikes you physically, or spending time alone working on your self-esteem? If you said the former, then you have some serious issues to work out with a therapist.

Reason #3: You Have Selective Hearing

Imagine that your partner has just told you the following: "You're a no-good piece of %@#&! You can't do anything right! You're so stupid—you'll never amount to anything! I don't even know why I love you!" If you ignored everything but the "I love you," then you've got selective hearing.

My point here is that you need to listen carefully to *every single word* that your partner says to you because it all means something. It's unwise to disregard nasty remarks and make the excuse that they "didn't really mean it." If they said it, then on some level they meant it! (And yes, this applies even in the heat of battle.)

Reason #4: You Fantasize
That the Abuse Will Just Stop

We all hope for positive things. For example, I tend to believe that all people have the potential to be good and kind; and I also believe in giving second chances when someone has made a mistake (with certain exceptions). This is a very dangerous attitude, however, when dealing with an abusive partner.

Most research indicates that once a pattern of emotional or physical abuse has started, it tends to be self-perpetuating; that is, the longer it's allowed to continue, the longer it *will* continue. After all, if you continue to take it, what incentive is there for your partner to stop? So heed this advice: You're playing Russian roulette with your life. You can't afford to keep living in the little fantasy world you've constructed in your head. Wake up and see your partner for who they are—a person with significant psychological problems who will take you both down.

Reason #5: You Believe That a Relationship Failure Means *You* Are a Failure

I once had a patient who wouldn't leave her abusive husband because she didn't want to be seen in their community as a "failure." It was important for her to maintain the façade of happiness to avoid the embarrassment that would result from the relationship breaking apart. Her husband knew this, so he got a free pass to cut her down on a daily basis and occasionally hit her.

In her mind, this was a small price to pay, for she could continue to maintain a certain image for her friends and family. She took the abuse for years—even I couldn't convince her to leave. Nor would she get the police involved, even after she'd received several serious injuries and feared for her own safety.

Even if your relationship isn't this bad, please always remember this: *You're not a personal failure if a relationship doesn't work out.* It's okay to admit a mistake and try again.

Reason #6: You Thrive on Conflict

Many couples stay together even as they spend their days literally beating each other up. They enter this warped dynamic where they feed off each other's rage, forging a bond based on distrust, anger, and abuse.

Conflict is sometimes exciting. If you don't believe that, think about the number of people who watch reality shows on TV and attend boxing matches, hockey games, and auto races. Some people just don't like to paddle in calm waters.

I used to believe that if only couples like this could just see themselves being so ugly to each other, they'd immediately stop the pattern of abuse. But then I realized that the cycle feeds on itself—the more they fight, the more they *need* to fight to regain control and the upper hand. It's as if they have a secret death wish to slowly destroy each other.

If this describes you and your partner, the best thing for you *both* is to break this cycle.

Reason #7: You Stay with an Abuser "for the Kids"

I've had many heated arguments with various individuals (including therapists) on this point over the years, for some people actually believe that children deserve to have two parents in the home, even if one abuses the other. You may have bought into the "family values" paradigm that it's better for children to have two parents at home—*no matter what*—than to grow up with a single parent. This is so wrong. You see, your children will learn how the world works based on what they *see*. You're the main teacher for your kids, whether you like it or not. And this means that whatever *you* decide to accept will become the norm for them.

So, even though your children may never observe the actual abuse you're getting, they'll eventually sense the effect it has on you. For example, your demeanor will change if you're always worried about when you're going to get beaten up again. And you'll also be telling your kids that it's okay to stay with someone who mistreats them—that they should tolerate being insulted, put down, or hit. Is this the legacy you want to pass down to your children?

Having said that, I understand the incredibly difficult decision you have to make. There's a very real chance that your children will suffer psychological damage regardless of whether you stay or go. You'll have to answer questions such as: "Where did Daddy go?" "Why aren't you together anymore?" "Did I do something wrong to make Daddy leave?" and "Why was Daddy hitting you and calling you names?"

These are tough questions to which you need to come up with good answers. But more important is sending the message to your children that it's *never* right to mistreat another being (human or animal).

Yes, I feel that it's preferable to raise your children on your own instead of staying with an abusive partner. I know it won't be easy, but you'll be doing the right thing for them in the long run.

Reason #8: You Absolutely Will Not Consider Divorce

If you have some aversion to divorce due to religious or moral beliefs, I commend you for your convictions. And if your partner turns on you in a physically or emotionally abusive manner, it surely will be a test of your faith. I honestly have to tell you that if your beliefs preclude divorce or separation, I don't have a great solution for you. Perhaps you should both go to your church for counseling and see if things can be resolved. If not, your life will be filled with conflict.

Reason #9: Things Will Actually Get Worse If You Try to Leave the Abusive Partner

If your partner has a really severe personality disorder, they may try to prevent you from leaving the relationship. There are various ways to do this:

- Your partner tells you that no one else will ever want you.

- When you try to leave the abuser, they hurt you even more.

- The abuser threatens to stalk you and harm any future partners.

- The abuser destroys things of great value to you (such as keepsakes, photos, and so forth); if they're really deranged, they may try to harm your children or even take them from you.

Remember that the abuser really needs you to stick around so that they can continue to live out their sick cycle of violence. They need you to be a receptacle for all the punishment they dish out. It's vitally important that you find a way to leave. You may have to do it in secret and move quickly (the element of surprise is critical here). And you should go to the police—they'll help you find a safe place to live and get a restraining order against your partner if you need it. The bottom line is that you need to utilize any and all weapons at your disposal in order to avoid retribution from the abuser.

I don't underestimate the level of commitment you're going to need to take these drastic steps. It may be one of the most courageous moves that you'll ever make . . . but it will also save your life.

Reason #10: You Get to Play Martyr

Many victims will stay with an abuser because, on some level, they're getting something out of the interaction. Now I'm not saying that they enjoy the abuse, but abusive behavior is a form of attention (granted, it's negative, but it's still attention, nonetheless).

Friends and family will often run to the rescue, trying to convince the victim to get out of the relationship. Here's where the martyr syndrome comes in. Some victims think they're exhibiting signs of courage when they get beaten up and then stay for more. It's like they're trying to show the world that they can "take it." This generates a lot of sympathy and shows of support—again, a lot of attention comes their way, and they get to be in the center of the storm.

I don't think there's anything courageous about remaining in an abusive situation—in fact, it's actually a sign of weakness. Eventually, when others realize that nothing they say has any impact on the victim's decisions, the support will dry up. Family and friends will tire of hearing about the abuse, and then the victim will truly be alone.

You must resist the urge to assume this role. I know that it feels nice to rally support from others, but this is only temporary. At the end of the day, you're still the one who's being abused.

♦ ♦ ♦

You must accept the fact that a partner who abuses you in any way will most likely continue the cycle unless *you* stop it. I know it can be extremely difficult to separate from an abuser because you still may have deep feelings for them. But show *yourself* some love by getting out of this situation. Then you can find a relationship that's based on mutual respect and kindness . . . with someone who will love you without degrading your character.

CHAPTER 14

ANNOYING
HABITS

Not all relationship problems are as heavy as anger and abuse issues. So let's change gears and lighten up a bit.

Now I'm sure that most of your partner's annoying habits aren't severe enough to end the relationship. However, many marriages and serious commitments *have* ended because the two people couldn't stand each other's little idiosyncrasies. For example, I knew someone who dumped her partner because he insisted on clipping his toenails in bed. She told him she was going to leave if he did it just one more time, which he did . . . and she packed her bags. This seems ridiculous, but she viewed the whole thing a matter of respect. As she told me, "If I can't depend on him to stop *this* stupid habit, what will he do next to annoy me?"

This chapter was tough for me to write, since I personally don't have any annoying tendencies. Just ask my wife . . . on second thought, don't ask her—you may get an earful. But somehow, Betsy and I have managed to get along living under the same roof for several years. We're living proof that when you commit to another person, you also commit to dealing with all of their foibles.

You name the repulsive habit, and I've undoubtedly heard it described on my radio show over the years. So I think we should begin here by acknowledging that *all* of us engage in personal practices that might seem perfectly acceptable to us, but which really get under our partner's skin.

I don't intend to list every possible nasty habit or lapse in personal hygiene—that would be impossible. But I *will* attempt to give you a road map to follow as you try to put up with your partner's bad breath, bad body odor, bad attire. . . . I can't guarantee total success, but at least you'll be able to develop a game plan for dealing with your partner's shortcomings after you read this chapter.

Problem #1: Your Partner Has a Habit That Really Annoys You

My wife can't stand it when I get out of the shower without drying off first. I track water on her side of the bathroom, which starts her day off wrong. For some reason, I like to be over by the sink when I towel off; however, I heard this complaint so many times that I gave up, and now (much to my chagrin), I dry myself while standing in the shower stall. I don't like it, but Betsy's much happier at the breakfast table.

On the other hand, I absolutely hate it when I get in our car and find the seat jammed up almost into the steering wheel. Betsy apparently likes to drive sitting perfectly upright—I don't see how she has any room, but that's her driving style. So I pointed out that I have trouble actually getting *in* the car unless the seat is pushed back. I'm sure that she doesn't think it's a big deal; in fact, she once asked me, "Why can't you just push it back yourself? It only takes a few seconds." I replied, "So then it would only take a few seconds for you to do it for me!" She tries to remember now, so things in that area have improved.

Okay, so maybe in the big scheme of things these habits won't lead to divorce. But if my wife and I hadn't both made the conscious decision to change, we'd be walking through our days feeling irritated and angry. This example illustrates that no matter how much you love your partner, one of these days you'll look at your significant other and exclaim in horror, "I can't believe you just did that!"

Obviously, I can't tell you what's annoying—it's up to you to define which of your partner's idiosyncrasies are absolutely intolerable. I'm sure that you've already got something in mind—that one particular thing they do that makes your teeth grind. So what do you do—argue over something trivial, or just live with it?

Solution #1

The answer to these questions is a resounding "maybe." At times it may not be worth it to get bent out of shape over your partner's driving habits, their tendency to leave the toothpaste cap off, or their fondness for having the same casserole five nights a week. However, if you just can't take it anymore, then it's time for action. You owe it to yourself to speak up and let it be known that there are a few things you'd like them to "work on."

Here's a step-by-step action plan to address an annoying habit:

— *Step 1*: Tell your partner that there's something you need to talk about, and you hope that they'll just listen without getting offended. Obviously, there's a good chance that your partner will take your constructive criticism the wrong way, especially if the behavior has been going on for years. If your husband has thrown his clothes in a heap on the bedroom floor since he was two, then he'll probably do anything he can to hold on to this pattern. It feels good to him, so why should he give it up easily?

You must first specifically define the offending action. This is no time to be vague—the more details the better so there's no confusion. You don't want to have the same conversation a month later after your partner says, "Gee, I thought I could still throw my clothes on the floor, just in a different room."

And be sure to give your partner a chance to respond while you listen to their side of the story.

— *Step 2*: Tell your partner how their behavior makes you feel and that it's a turnoff. There may still be some resistance, so you might have to pull out the heavy artillery. You have every right to ask, "Why won't you try to change if this is so important to me?" If you really want to use your might, you can go further by asking them, "Do you want me to be totally turned off by you?" A lot of sex lives are ruined because one person doesn't make the effort to look appealing for their significant other. So, if this is impacting your life together, your partner needs to know it.

— *Step* 3: Express that you'll be watching for accountability and will note each time the offending behavior is repeated. I know this sounds as if you're their mother, but consistency will make the difference in eradicating the behavior. If you take a stand but then let your partner slide by without consequences, your entire plan will be ruined.

If they slip up, say, "We spoke about this before, so I'd really appreciate it if you could be considerate." Acknowledge how hard it is to modify a chronic pattern—don't get emotional and yell, for objectivity and calmness are still the keys to getting what you want.

— *Step* 4: Give lots of praise when the behavior stops, for your partner needs to know that you're pleased and that you appreciate their efforts. Some people might get mad and resume the annoying habit if they get nothing in return, so it's critical to acknowledge the change.

During this process, it's also a good idea to ask your partner if there's anything *you* do that bothers them. They deserve the right to turn the tables on you, so listen to them without judgment! If the process is a give-and-take, then there will be a much greater chance for success. So try to change your own annoying habits as a courtesy, and as a gesture of goodwill.

♦ ♦ ♦

Problem #2: Your Partner Refuses to Change

You went through all of the steps correctly, yet your partner just keeps on as if you'd never had a conversation about modifying the situation. No matter how much you complain, they continue engaging in their irritating habit. You're being shown a total lack of respect. It's as if your partner is thumbing their nose at you, saying, "I'm just going to keep on doing it. What are you going to do *now?*"

This shifts the matter into another realm—the annoying habit has becomes less important than your partner's lack of respect. If your partner really cared about your feelings, they'd try really hard to please you. Once in a while they might forget and mess up, which is understandable, since giving up their habit may be like losing an old friend.

But if they don't put forth *any* effort at all, this indicates deeper problems with their personality and your relationship in general. Being ignored is hurtful, and living with a partner who does things that disgust you isn't going to work. This is a no-win situation for both of you—the more you complain, the deeper your partner will dig in. It will seem as if your partner is a child who's screaming, "You can't make me do anything! I'll do whatever I want!"

Solution #2

This behavior will force you to make a decision: Are you resigned to live a life filled with annoyance, or are you willing to end the relationship? You can't regard this as a decision about one little habit—this minimizes the whole issue. It's now a matter of disrespect and concern for your feelings.

You must find a way to communicate to your partner that you're both entering a treacherous area in your relationship. They'll probably try to make you feel petty for arguing about something that's "no big deal" and tell you that you're being selfish and bratty. Of course, this is their attempt to derail the conversation and place the blame on you.

Don't fall for it. You must express how unhappy it makes you when you're feeling unsupported and disrespected. If you break up, if won't matter if your partner tells his or her friends that you ended it over something "dumb." You'll know the truth . . . and so will they.

◆ ◆ ◆

It's natural for your significant other to occasionally do things that you think are irritating or ridiculous. Your temptation may be to yell and nag and try to win them over to your side (which you feel is the "better" way). But sometimes you're just going to have to accept the fact that even though your partner does things differently, their approach isn't necessarily wrong. Ask yourself whether you're attempting to make your partner do things your way for the sake of your ego. If this is the case, maybe it's time to celebrate the fact that we can all contribute in different ways—maybe their method is actually better. Why not at least give them the opportunity?

CHAPTER 15

HOUSEHOLD CHORES

When you live with your significant other, it isn't all wine and roses and romance—somebody has to clean the toilets and throw out the garbage!

Do you think that anyone really has fun doing household chores? Maybe there are a few compulsively neat people around who actually enjoy them, but most of us avoid such activities like the plague, while we secretly hope that someone else will do our "dirty work."

Fantasizing that someone will come along and be your personal maid or butler is all well and good, but reality is going to hit you sooner or later. You're going to have to pitch in and help out with household duties for the following reasons:

1. It's the right thing to do. It's simply not fair to expect your partner to take care of all the undesirable tasks while you get off scot-free.

2. Laziness will only breed resentment on the part of the partner who does all the work.

3. Being an equal in a committed relationship means that you volunteer to do equal amounts of the work.

I hated doing chores as a kid, and I still hate them as an adult. But I love my wife too much to pawn all the grunt work off on her. She didn't get married to become my mother . . . which she's reminded me of many times over the years.

I can tell you from personal experience that all kinds of personality flaws will pop up when two people debate the relative amount of housework each one does. That's because we all tend to overestimate the time and energy we spend on tasks we don't enjoy. For example, a friend of mine told me that it takes him a good hour a day to wash the dishes. Since he's only cleaning for two people, I don't think this is humanly possible—I mean, how many plates can he and his wife use?

Also, when undesirable work is involved, it seems as if other activities take on an immediate urgency. For example, when there's vacuuming to be done, I'll suddenly remember several errands outside the home I need to run. In fact, one of the lightbulbs in our house has been burned out for months, and I haven't changed it because, well, I was writing a book, I was working at a hospital, I was too tired, I just didn't get to it . . . none of which changed the fact that it's been dark in that closet for a long time.

You need to develop a system to figure out how to split up work around the house. And you shouldn't automatically assume that the woman will do all the cooking and cleaning. That's old school—you need to stop living in the '50s and enter the 21st century. Successful relationships are made up of two partners who are *both* willing to help out.

Once again, this chapter's structure deviates slightly from the others in that there are no problems and solutions, just a list of agreements for you and your partner to make. Hopefully, they'll help make this subject as palatable as possible.

Agreement #1:
Household Chores Will Be Split Fairly

The best way to divide up the work is obviously right down the middle. If you determine that there are 20 household jobs that need to accomplished in a week, then it's easy—you do 10 and your partner does the other 10. If you and your partner can agree to such an even split, great . . . if not, read on.

Agreement #2: Each List of
Jobs Will Be Given Equal Weight

One person shouldn't have to take on all the difficult chores while the other gets off easy. For instance, if you get to dust the furniture while your partner has to go out and weed the garden, then there's a relative difference in the time and energy each person is expending. You can go about remedying this problem in one of two ways:

1. Divide the chores evenly so that each person has some tough jobs and some that aren't so demanding.

2. Draw up an "easy" list and a "hard" list that
    are rotated between you and your partner on
    a daily or weekly basis (depending on the
    frequency of work needed).

Agreement #3: To Avoid Monotony, Housework Will Be Rotated Between the Two of You

My wife and I take turns deciding what to have for dinner, and then whoever cooks that night is responsible for cleaning up. We also try to rotate cleaning tasks: one week I scrub the floors and clean the kitchen and bathrooms, while she vacuums and dusts; the next week we reverse the jobs. This seems to work well, as neither of us gets burned out doing the same old chores over and over.

Agreement #4: You'll Stop Complaining about Housework

Whining about your tasks certainly won't improve morale in your relationship. A lot of couples start to blame each other when the house is dirty or there's garbage to be dealt with. Accept that you're going to generate some mess. It's a fact of life—even the cleanest person on the planet can't avoid dust, dirt, and germs. So acknowledge that you and your partner both make messes, which you both need to clean up.

Agreement #5: You Won't Procrastinate

Do you actually think that the garage will clean itself or the lawn will magically get mowed in the middle of the night? Sure, we all have a tendency to put off tasks that aren't fun, but when things pile up for weeks, it becomes that much harder to catch up. That's why I feel that doing one thing at a time is a heck of a lot simpler than trying to do everything at once. After all, "later" doesn't equate to "easier."

Agreement #6: You'll Set Aside a Regular Time for Chores

A haphazard time schedule will only lead to chores being left undone, so it will work much better if you and your partner set a definite time each day or week to get the job done. If you can make and keep appointments at work, why shouldn't you be able to fit household jobs into a schedule as well? You can even write them in your planner—if someone else sees that you schedule housework they may think that you're a bit strange, but so what? At least you'll rest assured that *your* home is a clean one!

Agreement #7: When an Emergency Arises, You'll Both Help Out

I know that this veers off our topic slightly, but things will come up without warning to knock you off your schedule. Maybe you'll have to work long hours one week, or you become ill—either way, your household tasks will get put on the back burner while you deal with more important matters. I certainly hope that your significant other will agree to pitch in and keep things going around the house until everything stabilizes.

This category also encompasses those situations in which there are more severe challenges in your household.

For example, some friends of mine have a child with significant and persistent health problems, which has caused sleepless nights, huge medical bills, and emotional and physical strain on them both. Yet they've survived the ordeal because both of them help out with their child equally and also share the other work involved in daily living. My point here is that if one partner is ill, out of town, disabled, or preoccupied with other family matters, then the other person needs to pick up the slack. If you're not willing to do this for the person you love, then what are you doing in a committed relationship in the first place?

◆ ◆ ◆

The common theme in all of these agreements is a spirit of generosity and fairness. There are several ways you can show your partner you love them—flowers and candlelit dinners are nice, but more important is doing something each day to make their life a little easier. This is a selfless way of living. If, however, you expect your significant other to spend their life catering to you and cleaning up your messes, then you're simply exhibiting arrogant and inconsiderate behavior.

Helping with the workload is a loving gesture. It may not be as flashy as a new piece of jewelry or a night out on the town, but it's just as important.

■ ■ �◇ O ◇ ■ ■

CHAPTER 16

CAREERS
AND TIME
MANAGEMENT

I recently met up with a good friend who seemed tired and frustrated. His life had taken a dramatic turn because he'd gotten married, started a new job, and become the proud father of twin girls . . . all in the span of a single year. As you might imagine, his daily routine had been greatly affected as he tried to balance the demands of his home life with the responsibility of being the family's breadwinner. The pressure was building, his work was suffering, and he and his wife were starting to snap at each other.

As we talked, I was reminded of the first truth about careers and relationships: *It's almost impossible to compartmentalize work stress and relationship stress, since trouble at home can mean trouble with your work, and vice versa.*

Luckily, my friend and his wife didn't want their marriage to buckle under the strain, so they decided to have a discussion about the difficulties of balancing work and a relationship. I hope that this chapter will help you and your significant other do the same. (Also note that I've included time-management issues here, since it's nearly impossible to separate out time spent in a relationship without considering time spent on the job.)

So let's define some problems that can be overcome in order to bring your relationship and career into perfect harmony.

Problem #1: Your Partner Doesn't Understand Your Career Goals

It's pretty rare for two people to have the same exact career goals. Even a couple who works together in the same field and sees each other during the day may have two very different agendas. Here are some of the permutations of mismatched career goals:

- Partner A is highly motivated at work, while Partner B stays at home.

- Partner A works at a certain pace, but Partner B thinks they should push harder.

- Partner A is willing to relocate for their job, but Partner B isn't.

- Partner A likes to put in long hours and save money, while Partner B likes to spend money and have fun.

- Both partners work hard yet have completely different career aspirations.

Any of the above situations has the power to end a relationship quickly, but this can be avoided if the couple is willing to work together to remedy their situation.

Solution #1

There's one surefire way to improve your odds here. Early in the relationship, let your potential partner know what your ambitions truly are. Honestly lay your career goals on the table—that way there won't be any surprises down the road for your partner, and you can also evaluate whether or not you and this person are compatible in terms of life values and goals. Naturally, things will happen in life that you can't foresee—you may lose your job, get transferred, or obtain a promotion that requires longer hours—but at least you'll have a pretty good idea where you stand with your partner if you've had a lengthy discussion before you get serious.

Once you've committed to someone, you need to sit down and begin to compromise (yep, there's that word again) with respect to your careers. You may need to make some concessions, but that's part of dedicating yourself to another person. Ambition is a great quality, but don't allow it to interfere with your life. After all, a job can only make you so happy, while your relationship is what really counts in the long run. Of course, once in a while you may still need to work long hours, miss a party or night out, or have to say no due to your work schedule—but you need to make your relationship the number-one priority and stop shortchanging your partner out of quality time together.

♦ ♦ ♦

Problem #2: You Hate Your Job
and Take It Out on Your Partner

I think that this dynamic is pretty self-explanatory, because hating your job will affect your home life—there are no two ways about it. Many arguments begin not because two people are unhappy with each other, but because one of them is fed up with things at work. I've counseled many couples whose lives revolve around how much they hate their jobs, which then spills over into their relationships. Career and relationship become synonymous; therefore, disliking the job comes to symbolize disliking the relationship.

Solution #2

You need to make the effort to separate frustration at work from what's going on at home. Here's a two-step approach that will work:

— *Step 1:* Direct your anger toward the appropriate people. Of course you'll feel like venting to your significant other, but they're really helpless when it comes to solving your career dilemmas, so it won't help to subject them to endless diatribes about your job. It's *your* responsibility to be an adult and stand up for yourself at work. And whenever you argue with your partner after a hard day, ask yourself, "Is this really an issue between us, or am I projecting my frustration about work onto my partner?"

— *Step 2:* It's imperative that you at least try to find a career that can satisfy you professionally. I mean, I think it would be awfully arduous to wake up each day absolutely dreading your job. I know it isn't easy, but changing careers could preserve your relationship *and* your sanity.

◆ ◆ ◆

Problem #3: There's No Line of Separation Between Work and Home

We all know workaholics . . . but, to be honest, I'm not one of them. I'm often asked how I leave my patients' problems at the office; in fact, my wife and friends have commented that I generally don't talk about my work at all when I'm at home. Do I have some magical ability that allows me to compartmentalize areas of my life so neatly? Well, no . . . but I do know a few tricks that I'll share with you.

Solution #3

One of the keys to keeping things in your relationship in perspective is the ability to set boundaries on the job and at home. This means that you can't give in to your boss every time you're asked to stay late, causing you to miss quality time with your partner; but on the flip side, you also can't blow off work or show up late because your partner wants you to. Here's a statement that will work in both situations: "No, I need to attend to other things that are also important right now."

Your success in this area will ultimately be based on *flexibility*. You and your partner must always allow room for negotiation—there may be times when you have to work long hours on a big project and put your relationship on the back burner for a while; other times you may need a long-overdue vacation, a sick day, or a personal day to hang out with your partner. This is all part of the balancing act.

In addition, you should make a distinct separation between work and home. For example, on my drive to and from work, I play some relaxing music. I don't spend this time on my cell phone tieing up loose ends or returning messages—I do all that before I ever walk out of my office. I try very hard to finish my work before I leave for the day, even if this means that I stay for a few extra minutes. This is great for my marriage, because once I walk in the door to my house, I'm "home." This way, I'm able to create two distinct halves in my day . . . and I get some time to myself as well.

Here are some other techniques that work to separate work from home:

- Run some errands after work to get your mind on other tasks.

- Exercise—it clears your head and works off excess energy and frustration.

- Schedule a class or hobby right after your workday so that you're focused on something you enjoy when you walk in the door to your home.

- If you work at home, make sure that you've set aside a specific room just for work. If you're not working, then don't go in there! And remember, when you're done for the day, leave your home for a while—go for a walk or run some errands, but do something to buffer your work and home time.

One more thing: Do not, and I repeat, *do not*, attempt to solve your relationship problems while you're at work.

If I had a dime for every time I had to listen to a co-worker argue with their partner on the phone, I'd be a very rich man. There seems to be no limit to the sordid tales I've heard—stories of cheating and lying, sexual improprieties, and a variety of other intimate problems. What's funny is that nothing ever seems to get resolved this way, since after a heated exchange the phone usually gets slammed down in a fit of anger. Relationship issues need to be addressed face-to-face, not over the phone at work! In addition, stop sharing details about your relationship with your co-workers—this is something that I guarantee you'll regret.

The lesson here is this: *When you're at work, focus on work.* Conversely, when you get home, try to avoid extensive conversations about the stressful day you had.

◆ ◆ ◆

Problem #4: Your Partner
Doesn't Spend Enough Time with You

One of the most common complaints that women have about men is that they don't spend enough time working on the relationship. Women have had this issue with men for as long as relationships have been around, and it probably won't change anytime soon.

I included this problem in this chapter because many people use work as an excuse to stay away from home. In order to avoid chores, kids, or their partners, some people will "stay late at the office" or "meet with clients" during the evenings. I knew a guy who worked on a "big project" night after night, when in reality he was out drinking with his friends and ignoring his family. If this describes your partner, what can you do?

Solution #4

First determine how much time you require with your partner without any outside interruptions. If you feel neglected, speak up so your partner knows there's a problem. You can say something like, "I really want to be around you more. How can we work together so we can have more alone time?" Then offer to make some concessions and expect the same in return.

For example, offer to meet your partner at their workplace occasionally for lunch or dinner. Look into some hobbies and activities that you'll both enjoy. Try to plan at least one "date night" every week—I truly believe that this is one of the most important things you can do for your relationship, since you'll get to reconnect on a regular basis. Before you know it, you'll have all the quality time you need with your partner!

◆ ◆ ◆

Problem #5: Your Partner Can't or Won't Work

Some people can't work due to a disability, so their partner may need to provide all the financial support. Many relationships thrive under these conditions, though, because both people contribute to the relationship in some way.

But what happens if your partner decides that they don't *want* to work anymore? Perhaps they're pregnant, taking time off to regroup, or going back to school to change careers—all of which could actually strengthen your relationship in the long run. However, if your partner's unemployment is due to less noble reasons (they'd rather kick back, they can't hold a job, or they've simply become dependent on you for financial support), then it will ultimately cause a huge strain in the relationship.

Solution #5

The decision you make will be based on how much you're willing to stand. If everything's crumbling around you and you're on the verge of bankruptcy, then it seems obvious that you wouldn't be able to tolerate your partner's refusal to work. If your financial situation is stable, but your partner seems content living off what you make, then you need to determine whether this is acceptable to you. If it isn't, then it's up to you to tell them how you feel. Hopefully, you'll make some headway and your partner will realize how important it is for them to pull their own weight.

Unfortunately, you can't force someone to be productive in the world. I had to learn this the hard way. My intense drive to work on ten different things at once is difficult to match, so I needed to learn to back off from pressuring my wife, and give her a chance to do her own thing. However, if we were really in a bad way financially and Betsy adamantly refused to do anything to help, I'd probably be really disappointed and question her commitment to our relationship.

♦ ♦ ♦

It may be useful to pretend you're on a seesaw, trying to balance your career and your relationship. If you *do* find that perfect equilibrium, your self-esteem *and* your relationship will flourish.

■ ■ ◊ O ◊ ■ ■

CHAPTER 17

FAMILY
AND IN-LAWS

When you commit to another person, you also enter into relationships with their relatives. It doesn't matter if you're dating, engaged, married, straight, or gay—almost everyone has a family somewhere, and these people will now be a major part of your life, whether you like it or not.

Whenever I think of in-laws, I'm always reminded of the movie *Meet the Parents,* which my wife and I love. Now I'm sure that you won't have to encounter any of the fiascos that happen to the main character as he gets to know his future wife's parents, but your "second family" *will* have their own idiosyncrasies and issues that you'll have to deal with.

I've been really lucky in this department—I get along really well with my wife's parents, and we've had some great times together. I hope you enjoy the same camaraderie with your own relatives; if you don't, you're going to need a good strategy to survive.

Let's take a look at some of the more common family problems that can greatly affect your relationship, as well as some solutions that can work to defuse tense situations.

Problem #1: Your In-Laws Interfere in Your Relationship

You should make every effort to treat your partner's parents and other family members with respect, but if they love to meddle in your affairs, you may feel as if your brain is swimming from all their unwanted advice. They tell you how to raise your children, where to live, what house to buy, when to take vacations, and so forth. Even if you remind yourself that they mean well, how can you handle their constant butting in?

Solution #1

You and your partner must ultimately be in charge of your relationship and strive to make decisions independently. This, however, can often be easier said than done.

One of the things I get asked most is: "How do I get my partner to stop listening to their parents all the time?" So many adults will do exactly what Mom or Dad tells them to do because they're afraid to stand up to them, or they feel guilty about opposing them.

If this is the case in your relationship, be prepared for a long and bloody battle. On some level, the parents may be angry that they gave up their son or daughter to you. Of course this isn't your fault, but parents always want to be number one. And when they perceive a threat to displace them, sparks can fly.

I propose the following plan of action when dealing with meddling in-laws:

— *Step 1:* Tell them that you're not trying to replace them in the eyes of your partner. This may relieve some of the tension.

— *Step 2:* Communicate to your partner that the two of you are now a team and must make all major life decisions on your own. Be open to accepting occasional advice and even criticism from the in-laws, but demand that your partner consult you and respect your wishes more than their parents'.

— *Step 3:* Once in a while, accept your in-laws' advice and go with it. This will make them feel more important and valued and will enhance your relationship with them.

— *Step 4:* Don't make the mistake early on of giving your partner the ultimatum of "it's them or me!" You may soon find out that blood is thicker than water as you're unceremoniously dumped. Later on, when your relationship is solid and serious, you'll have enough clout and leverage to insist that *you're* now number one for your partner.

◆ ◆ ◆

Problem #2: Your In-Laws Don't Like You

You may have little control over this one. Your in-laws could dislike you for a number of crazy reasons, none of which may have anything to do with your personality or character. Although fathers can be just as guilty in this department, the usual culprits here are the mothers. So let's say that your partner's mother is upset that

you're in the picture. She tries to minimize your importance by shutting you out of family functions, mocking
your wishes, or one-upping you in the domestic department (cooking, shopping, gift buying, and so forth). And
when you turn to your partner for moral support, you find
that he or she is so scared of her that no action is taken.
What can you do?

Solution #2

First of all, you must decide early on that you'll do anything within reason to have a good relationship with your
in-laws. Smile a lot, don't make any major waves, go to
family functions, and try not to stick out too much. Arguing with them won't help your situation and may turn them
against you even more. Having said that, they shouldn't
be allowed to treat you poorly.

If your in-laws are openly hostile toward you, try asking them if you've done anything to offend them. This tactic may work, but you may also be met with: "No, there's
no problem. We like you a lot"—followed by no change in
their behavior.

If they continue to treat you unkindly, then it's time
to sit down with your partner and ask for help. If they
refuse, then you need to question their level of commitment to you (as well as their ability to separate from their
family).

Finally, and I hate to say this at the risk of sounding
trite, just live your life. Do things that you enjoy, and
make sound decisions based on your own intuition. If your
in-laws don't like it, well, too bad. Maybe someday they'll
come around and appreciate you, or maybe they won't—
but basing your self-esteem around what they think will
do you no good. Get your support from others who will
truly back you without judgment and criticism.

◆ ◆ ◆

Problem #3: Your In-laws
Want You to Ignore Your Own Family

This problem tends to rear its ugly head the most during the holidays. A typical couple has two sets of people to visit on every special occasion—but with the high rate of divorce in this country, you could be looking at *four* sets of relatives to visit! That's certainly a lot of turkey and presents.

Some in-laws, however, demand that you see *only* them. They want you to blow off your own family, which makes them feel special and in control. But how far can you be pushed? How much will you let them control your actions?

Solution #3

I can't stress enough that *you and your partner must be unified on this issue.* Decide on a schedule of visitation, and make a pact that you won't cave in to either set of parents. Try to be with everyone as equally as possible, given the limitation of geography. If you have children, it's important to involve the grandparents as much as you can. Not only is this healthy for your kids, it's also a family bonding experience that can benefit everyone.

◆ ◆ ◆

Problem #4: Your Partner
Can't Cut the Apron Strings

Many people go into adulthood with unresolved childhood conflicts; consequently, they're still attached to domineering and controlling parents and can't seem to break free. For example, I once treated someone who would go to his parents' house every night to eat dinner, have his laundry done, and hang out in his old room watching TV . . . despite the fact that he had a wife and two children waiting at home! I told him up front that he was irresponsible and selfish to ignore his family this way, but he complained that his mother would throw a fit if he didn't visit her nightly. I responded that he shouldn't have gotten married if he didn't plan to be around. Apparently he agreed, because he and his wife divorced shortly thereafter.

I'm not suggesting that your situation is this severe, or that you and your partner should completely avoid your respective parents again after you form a relationship. But how can you separate from your parents *and* live your lives as adults?

Solution #4

The following point needs to be clarified early in your relationship: *Your bond together is now the most important thing in your lives.* Of course your parents can be a part of your life together, but they're no longer your priority. After all, a parent's prime job is to prepare their child for adulthood and then let go so they can form relationships of their own.

It's time to let go of your mother and father as caretakers and see them as a support system. If your partner can't seem to let go of their parents, you need to demand more time together and some cooperation. There's nothing wrong with family vacations together, letting your kids spend time with Grandma and Grandpa, or the occasional dinner at Mom and Dad's—but you and your partner need to come first for each other.

♦ ♦ ♦

As the saying goes, "You can't choose your family." But I maintain that on some level you can, because you chose your partner. And, ultimately, this is the person you're sharing your life with now. Your families may not enjoy taking a backseat, but if you handle these situations correctly, your in-laws can come to accept their new place, and maybe even enjoy it.

CHAPTER 18

FRIENDS AND LEISURE

Friends and hobbies will have a huge influence on your relationship. As with any other outside interest, they can add some variety but can also detract from your relationship. In order to maintain balance, you and your partner should agree on the following:

- You can both have friendships outside of the relationship.

- You can choose your own friends. This means that you can't judge your partner's friends by your own criteria.

- You'll try to get to know each other's friends.

- You'll both pursue outside leisure activities whether the other person chooses to participate or not.

- You'll allow each other to grow in divergent areas, which will enhance your relationship.

- And finally, you'll both pursue these outside endeavors *in moderation*. This is usually the sticking point—it's not the hobby or friends in particular, it's the inordinate amount of time spent away from the relationship that causes arguments . . . which brings us to our first problem.

Problem #1: Your Partner Spends Too Much Time with Friends or on a Hobby

I don't know of a relationship that can survive if one partner is always spending time with friends or engaging in other activities outside of the home. This doesn't define a great love relationship; in fact, it signals that something is drastically wrong. Yet it *is* necessary to be able to pursue some things outside of the relationship. You can't be together 24 hours a day, 7 days a week, 52 weeks a year, or you'll drive each other nuts!

The difficulty with this particular problem is that your idea of time required pursuing outside interests may not gel with your partner's. And that's when the fights begin.

Solution #1

When you commit to a relationship, you're also committing a majority of your time and energy, so you may just have to give up some of your freedom. I'm not saying to bag all of your friends and hobbies, but the time you spend on these things will have to decrease now that you're a couple. Therefore, I think that a couple nights a week out with your friends is plenty of time to unwind from the relationship. And if your partner wants to take a vacation alone or with other friends or relatives without you, I don't see anything inherently wrong with this—as long as it's infrequent, they clearly state up front where they're going and how long they'll be gone, and they keep in touch with you periodically during their time away.

When a client of mine felt angry or stressed out, he used to go to a beach house in Florida for a week and not talk to his wife. I told him that this was a terrible coping skill that could end their relationship. He persisted, and I was right. His wife got tired of his rude behavior and left him.

On the other hand, my brother-in-law goes away for a golf weekend with friends once or twice each summer, leaving his wife to care for their kids. Since he calls her each day to check in, she's okay with these trips—and they may actually help the relationship, because husband and wife get a small break from one another and have the chance to regroup.

◆ ◆ ◆

Problem #2: Your Partner Has a Good Friend of the Opposite Sex

In an ideal world, you and your partner should be able to pick out friends without regard to gender. I really do believe that men and women can be platonic friends. In fact, I have plenty of female pals to whom I have absolutely no sexual attraction, and they feel the same about me. I can hang out with them because my wife is understanding and secure with our relationship. But I also have nothing to hide from her—I'm up front with Betsy, so there's certainly no call for her to get jealous.

It's perfectly fine to have friends of the opposite sex, but you should never do anything with them that you couldn't invite your partner to join in on. In other words, nothing should be done behind their back. And sex should never enter the picture—friends don't have sexual contact if they're involved in relationships with other people.

Solution #2

I believe you should allow your partner to have any friends they choose, as long as your trust is never broken. When it comes to exes, however, the water is a little murkier—of course it's theoretically possible to stay friends with someone whom you dated or married, but it's not very probable. Lingering sexual attraction or hurt feelings usually get in the way, and your partner may wonder why you feel the need to keep this person in your life (unless you have children together).

Your partner should introduce you to their friend as soon as possible so you can meet and get to know one another. This may defuse a lot of tension. If you're open with each other, your partner won't have to give up a cherished friendship.

♦ ♦ ♦

Problem #3: Your Partner
Takes Up Destructive Hobbies

I always joke with my wife that I'm going to take up smoking and drinking so I can have some real fun. There's nothing like a bad habit to inject a little excitement into a relationship. Okay, I'm just kidding, but potentially destructive interests *can* ruin relationships and lives.

What would happen if you partner proudly announced

one day that they'd started gambling, getting high on drugs, or frequenting prostitutes and strip clubs? This may sound unbelievable, but let me assure you that it's entirely possible. And problem friends sometimes go right along with the problem activities. Usually people won't take up something illegal or destructive on their own—friends have a way of persuading intelligent, conservative people to indulge in outrageous pursuits. So what should you do if you find yourself in this situation?

Solution #3

First, define the activities that you absolutely can't tolerate under any circumstances. If any of these things begins to occur in your relationship, you must take a stand and insist that your partner discontinue it at once. The longer you tolerate bad behavior, the more it will continue. If you let your partner go out several nights a week and not return home until morning, what makes you think that they're going to see the error of their ways on their own? This is no time to be soft—your future may be riding on your ability to put your foot down.

◆ ◆ ◆

Problem #4: Your Partner Doesn't Develop Any Outside Interests and Only Wants to Be with You

What if your partner *only* wants to concentrate on you? On the surface this would seem to be a great thing, as you get lavished with attention and love. Who doesn't want that?

You don't. Believe me, you don't want to be the sole focus of your partner. It will feel smothering and get old fast. A mature, healthy partner will balance time as a couple with time as an individual; in other words, they'll keep growing as a person. So your partner needs to keep some sense of individuality, rather than completely merging with you and your life.

Solution #4

When you first start dating someone, ask about their hobbies and friends. If you're met with a blank stare, or if the answer is "I only need you," the relationship could turn creepy very soon.

You should actively encourage your partner to keep seeing friends and enjoying outside hobbies and activities, while you do the same. This will add interest and variety to your relationship, especially if you've been together for any length of time.

If your partner refuses to pursue any interests outside of your relationship, then you need to decide whether you're willing to stay with an uninspired, dependent person who makes you feel trapped. If the answer is yes, then don't do anything—I'm sure this pattern will continue indefinitely. If the answer is no, then you may need to look elsewhere for someone with a little more get-up-and-go.

♦ ♦ ♦

Problem #5: You Two Have Nothing in Common

Other relationship experts have suggested that two people can bond for a lifetime even if they have no common interests or friends. I disagree—lust and a strong physical attraction can certainly draw people together, but it won't be enough to sustain a relationship over time. Problems will start up because you're interested in hobbies and leisure activities that your partner either hates or refuses to get involved in. If there's virtually nothing that you can share with your partner, then what will you do together for the rest of your lives?

Solution #5

The solution here is short and sweet: You need to ask questions while you're dating! It's better to find out that you're just two different people right away, instead of in a few years when the pain will be greater.

Honestly ask yourself, "Do we really want the same things out of life? Are we traveling on the same path? Do we enjoy some of the same outside interests? Do we have a similar taste in friends?"

Compatibility can't be forced. It's either there or it isn't in the relationship. Common interests and goals are simply an essential part of any good intimate relationship.

♦ ♦ ♦

The last thing I'd like to say here is that it's really true that you should be friends with your partner, first and foremost, and then everything else will follow. My wife is my best friend, and I hope that you can say the same about your significant other.

CHAPTER 19

DIVORCE AND OTHER BREAKUPS

You may be wondering why I'm including a chapter on failed relationships in this book. After all, the decision to divorce or break up is clearly made because it's determined that problems *can't* be solved.

Well, the reason is that I'd like you to think about several important things before and during the process of leaving another person, and I want you to know that there's a right way and a wrong way to do it. You're going to have to work through a tremendous amount of pain, and deal with your feelings of loss, before you can move on successfully. Divorce is especially difficult—particularly if you have kids or if you and your ex didn't split on the best of terms.

Instead of our old problem-and-solution format, in this chapter I'd like to suggest some ways to make the transition from "coupled" to "single" a bit easier.

Suggestion #1: Do Everything You Can to Save Your Relationship

There are unprecedented levels of divorce in the United States today. More than 50 percent of marriages break up, which means that the odds are greater that you *won't* end up being together till death do you part than that you will!

But I don't want you to give up easily—a marriage or relationship at least deserves that you give it your all to save it. Here's what you can do:

1. Sit down with your partner and tell them what you're feeling. If they're engaging in behavior that you can't tolerate, tell them that it must stop immediately.

2. If there's no change, tell your partner that their actions are endangering your relationship.

3. Insist that professional help (either singularly or together) is needed to work on a solution. Tell your partner that if this happens, your relationship has a chance of surviving.

4. If your partner refuses to acknowledge the problem or won't take any steps to correct it, you have every right to start the process to end the relationship.

5. Finally, try not to second-guess your ultimate decision. Yes, it will be difficult to leave your partner and end the relationship, but remember that you're doing it to ensure your future happiness.

You need to go through these five steps *in consecutive order* so that you don't make a rash decision. A serious breakup will affect the rest of your life, so careful consideration of the consequences is necessary. However, if something so terrible has happened that the relationship is now irrevocably broken—such as abuse (physical and/or emotional), infidelity, chronic lying, lack of sexual interest in the other, or destructive habits or addictions—then you need to dust yourself off and move on.

Suggestion #2: Create a Formal End to the Relationship

If the judge bangs down his gavel and proclaims that the marriage is over, then that's a pretty good way to formally end things. But many relationships don't end so neatly, so it can be difficult to get on with your life. Consequently, many people keep returning to old partners because of unfinished business—they continue to see each other just as "friends," or they still sleep together. I think that's a mistake.

Of course it's really painful to say good-bye to someone you once loved, but unless you definitively end your relationship, you won't be able to move on. Your grieving process will be much more difficult if your former partner is still hanging around. Moreover, you probably won't begin to date other people, since the fantasy that you can "still make it work" will be alive and kicking.

I suggest that you tell your ex the following: "I really need to move on. This is incredibly difficult for me, but we need to go on with our lives and not see or talk to each other for a while." This implies that you may come into contact again in the future, but it will also give you time to really separate from each other.

You must find the strength to make this break. Use friends and family for support, and take some time for yourself. And this is really important—if there are possessions to be split up or children to raise, then the separation *must* be handled in a legal fashion. (I'm always amazed when people try to arrange their own custody. Invariably, one person begins to slack off on visits or financial support, and the children are ultimately the ones who are hurt.)

Suggestion #3: Try to Remain Civil, Even If Your Feelings Are Hurt

Rejection hurts, and it brings out the worst in people. You may find yourself acting irrationally and doing things out of character, but please try to resist making public scenes or seeking revenge on the one who hurt you.

Anger and bitterness can consume people's lives, and these feelings won't make you feel better. I'm not saying that you shouldn't strongly express your sentiments to someone who got the best of you. If you need to tell them off, go for it. Get it out of your system, but then tell yourself that it's time to grieve your loss. This is the action that will help you the most. Focus energy on *yourself* instead of your ex. Relationship failures hurt, and you need to take time to deal with your feelings. It may take up to a year or so before you'll feel like going out and meeting new people again. This is perfectly acceptable. Don't bow to pressure from close friends and family members who want to speed you along—you need to go at your own pace.

The best revenge is moving on and finding happiness. Don't give someone you broke up with the power to ruin your life forever.

Suggestion #4: Be Kind to Yourself

This may sound clichéd, but so what? At the end of the day, the only person you have control over is *you*. You can't force anybody else to be nice to you, but when things get rough, you can make the conscious decision to be nice to yourself. Look at yourself in the mirror and say, "I'm okay. I really am. I pledge to do good things for myself that make me happy."

Then let yourself be a human being. Cry if you must, and talk about your pain with your family and friends. Before you know it, you'll laugh again and will even find someone else to bond with . . . and maybe that person will be the one you ultimately spend your life with. But until you properly deal with the emotions of your breakup and give yourself time to heal properly, you won't be ready for the happy and healthy relationship you deserve.

CHAPTER 20

DATING

M any people have no clue how to date well, which is too bad—especially if they expect to have a success-ful relationship. After all, it's the first step in the whole process!

There are tricks to making your dating experiences fun and productive, so consider these next few pages as a primer on dating. I believe that after you've read this chapter, you'll have a much better handle on what it takes to have great dates *and* overcome common problems in this area to boot. If you accept the following realities, you'll be a successful "dater" in no time!

Reality #1: Dating Is Difficult

Finding a love match is really hard. If you can't make things happen with another person, is there something wrong with you? Probably not. In fact, most of the factors deciding whether somebody will date you or not are out of your control—so give yourself a break! Maybe the person you're interested in is on the rebound, depressed, involved with someone else, or just having a bad day; or maybe your timing is wrong. This all means that, in addition to your sparkling personality, you'll need to have some luck on your side as you wade through the dating pool. And, yes, you're gong to have to kiss a lot of frogs. This leads us to the next reality.

Reality #2: You May Have to Date a Lot Before You Find the Right Person

Dating is like any other skill, so it may take some practice before you finally get it right. There's nothing wrong with meeting many new people—at least you'll get the sense of what you like and what turns you off. In other words, each unsuccessful dating experience is a slice of life that will help you define exactly what you want. I know that after you've been dumped it will be hard to think of it in this way, but try. Take some time to regroup, and then have the courage to start over again.

Reality #3: Be Yourself!

You can't hide your true personality forever—it will naturally come out sooner or later. You are who you are, so what's the point of trying to fool someone else?

Of course you and your date are going to put your best feet forward during your first few meetings, but if you act natural, you'll be able to see if there truly is any connection between you. This will save you both a lot of wasted time.

Reality #4: Great Dates Depend on Contributions from *Both* People

You don't deserve a second date if you just sit there and depend on the other person to carry the conversation and entertain you. Dating is an active process that will only be successful if both people make an effort. It isn't your date's responsibility to make the evening a memorable experience for you.

Many people are taught that their suitors should have the dates all planned out from beginning to end. This is a big mistake. Instead of adhering to this outdated belief, why don't *you* initiate some interesting conversation or suggest something creative for you both to do? This way, you won't look like a bump on a log, and your date will most likely appreciate your efforts.

Reality #5: A Date Should Be Used to Ask Questions and Size Up the Other Person

As you gaze across the table at your date, you find yourself dreamily thinking that they could be "The One," so you try not to be too forward or ask any upsetting questions. You don't really learn anything about this person's life . . . until later, when you find out that they drink a lot, are ostracized from their family, and like to cheat on their partners. Suddenly, you realize that you're in love with a real loser.

How could this happen? Well, you made a crucial mistake in not asking questions about this person's life early on. You didn't do your dating job, which is to find out as much as you can about that person so that there are no surprises down the road.

There's nothing wrong with curiosity. In fact, if your

date refuses to answer questions or acts offended, then you may be with someone who has some serious skeletons in their closet. The one question that I think is most important to ask during the first few dates is: "Why did your previous relationships fail?" Their answer will tell you a lot about how they handle failure, the types of people they like to get involved with, and how they attempt to solve problems. If they respond, "Oh, they just ended, that's all," press for more details. Nothing just "ends"—there are *always* reasons for relationship breakups.

Reality #6: While You're Dating Someone, Watch How They Treat Other People

I can't stress this enough: *If your date is rude to your friends, family members, or even total strangers, you can expect the same treatment at some point.*

You may overlook this behavior because your date tells you that "you're different from the rest." Don't buy it. You can't afford to live in a fantasy world in your quest to choose a partner for life. Open your eyes and see that the way your partner acts at their worst moments will eventually be directed at you. Is this what you want?

Reality #7: Too Much Attention May Drive Them Away

The person you're dating has their own life. Just because you're not together for an evening doesn't mean that they're out picking up other people. Yet it may be tempting to contact your date often, to let them know you care, to keep tabs on them, or to just hear their voice. But to continue doing this may get you dumped, because your date may feel that you're smothering them.

On the other hand, I once read a book that said one should never call a date back. This is incredibly stupid advice, since common courtesy dictates that calls should be returned. The bottom line is that you should just take it easy and go with the flow. This is easier said than done, I know—but desperation is never a strong selling point, at any stage of a relationship.

Reality #8: When Sex Enters the Picture, Your Relationship Will Change

Sex changes the dynamic of any relationship, it's that simple. It can bring two people closer together or can quickly lead to the end of the relationship. In fact, one of the most common questions I'm asked is: "When should I first sleep with someone?" I believe that sexual relations should only commence after you're pretty confident that the relationship will last and that you're not being used. Ultimately, this is something you'll probably feel in your gut, so you'll have to decide if the time is right and then go for it. I've known people who had sex on their first date and then went on to get married. I've seen others wait for years, only to have the relationship break up. So there's no absolute timetable for everyone.

Sex represents taking a chance in your relationship. If you've asked the right questions about your date's sexual history, you use protection, and you feel a real connection with each other, then your roll of the dice might be a successful one.

Reality #9: Long-Distance Relationships Are Almost Impossible to Pull Off

I know this one from experience. When I was in college, I tried to carry on a relationship with someone who lived a few hours away. We really did like each other, but every weekend we spent our time together fighting about petty issues. I finally figured out that we were simply trying too hard to make every moment together "special," since we wouldn't see each other again for a week. The relationship ultimately crumbled from the pressure.

This isn't unusual. Long-distance relationships are mysterious and exciting but difficult to maintain. After all, you can't really get to know someone if you only see them periodically. If your relationship has any chance of working, then at some point you must make the commitment to live in the same location (of course, there are exceptions to every rule).

I'd also like to take this opportunity to comment on Internet dating. A friend of mine met his wife on-line—but he also moved to her city, and they got to know each other quite well before they committed. They have a great chance of staying together. However, meeting people over the Internet can be very dangerous. People lie about themselves and misrepresent their lives—you really don't know whom you're chatting with. I implore you to at least be safe. Meet your new "e-buddy" in a very public place, and take a friend along.

Reality #10: You Need to Feel Comfortable in Order to Meet Another Person

Dating is a humbling experience that can take its toll on your self-esteem. For example, many people make the mistake of going out to places that make them uncomfortable because they're the happening "meat markets." I met my wife at a local bar/restaurant, but it was a place where we both felt at ease.

Now you may get lucky and bump into your soul mate on the street one day, like in the movies. But chances are, that's not going to happen. So the challenge for you is to define what you like to do and then go out and pursue these activities. You'll meet people with similar interests, and if you don't find anyone to date, you'll at least make new friends . . . and who knows who they'll introduce you to? After all, it's been said that most people meet their future spouses through mutual friends.

Reality #11: It Only Takes One

If you went out and asked ten people for a date and nine rejected you, you'd probably feel pretty lousy. Yet if just one said yes and you went on to have a terrific time, would it have been worth the effort?

My point here is that you may feel like giving up after a series of bad dates or rejections. But if your goal is to form a relationship that lasts, you can't afford to have this attitude. It's not going to work out with most of the people you date . . . but one successful date is all you need to get the ball rolling for a successful *relationship*.

This is one area I personally know a lot about. I became so frustrated with dating at one point that I decided to go on a "dating sabbatical." So for several months I didn't ask anyone out or try to get phone numbers when I went out with friends. Strangely enough, I felt better about myself during this time than when I was dating, and I developed other interests. And this story has a happy ending, because I met Betsy when I wasn't looking. Our dates just seemed to click, and the rest is history.

Reality #12: There's No Use Playing Dating Games

Playing games seems to be most people's m.o. out in the dating world—some people play hard to get, while others feel love for another person but won't say it out loud. This is a real shame—don't you think that your partner deserves to know how you really feel?

I admit that this is a matter of timing. It's probably not wise to profess your undying love to someone on the first date (that is, unless you want to see them flee as fast as they can!). But at some point, if you have loving feelings, you should share them. After all, it's possible that your partner feels exactly the same way you do, but is scared to admit it.

As I said before, the real you will eventually come out. Sharing and generosity will open the door for love and kindness to flow in both directions. Someone has to make the first move, so why not you?

◆ ◆ ◆

Believe me, I know how hard dating can be. But I think that with the right attitude of openness, honesty, and fun, you can easily attract a great date—who just may turn into something more.

GETTING YOUR NEEDS MET

It's simple: Relationships end because problems can't be solved. That's why I felt strongly enough to write an entire book on this topic. The common denominator behind every relationship problem is this: *If you or your partner has a need that isn't being met, it will turn into a problem for the relationship.*

When people don't get what they want, they get angry, complain, and do things to hurt their partner—they don't communicate, withhold sex, cheat, or engage in activities that can mortally wound the relationship. Consequently, both partners lose.

Before I wrap up this book, I think it's important to leave you with a specific plan to get your needs met. If you're disappointed with your partner, *you* must share some of the blame. Sure, it's easy to complain about somebody else; it's far more difficult to look back at your own actions and realize that you never adequately communicated what you wanted.

So it's about time that you took responsibility for your own life. Speak up—stop believing that your partner should just be able to read your mind. They can't, and it's completely unfair of you to ask them to.

Most relationship problems can be headed off at the pass if you follow this algorithm, which I presented in my first book, *A Relationship for a Lifetime.* This is the path to getting your needs met:

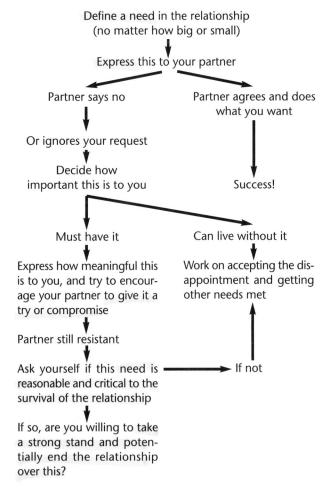

Define a need in the relationship
(no matter how big or small)

Express this to your partner

Partner says no

Partner agrees and does what you want

Or ignores your request

Decide how important this is to you

Success!

Must have it

Can live without it

Express how meaningful this is to you, and try to encourage your partner to give it a try or compromise

Work on accepting the disappointment and getting other needs met

Partner still resistant

Ask yourself if this need is reasonable and critical to the survival of the relationship

If not

If so, are you willing to take a strong stand and potentially end the relationship over this?

♦ ♦ ♦

I hope that you and your partner never encounter any obstacle that could take away from your love for each other. But I know that this goal is nearly impossible, since problems are an everyday reality in our lives. Part of the human experience is dealing with bumps in the road—perhaps this book has helped you navigate those bumps.

Successful couples make it look easy, as if they're floating on air across a crowded ballroom, dancing perfectly in step and noticing no one else. But to dance that beautifully, they've had to put in a lot of effort and time behind the scenes to get their act just right. Don't live your life being envious of such couples—join in the fun and create a little of your own relationship magic. Commit to a process of open communication, problem solving, and kindness each and every day.

I'm honored to have been your guide on this journey. I wish you the best of luck in your quest for a relationship filled with fun, love, mutual respect, and joy.

Kelly E. Johnson, M.D., the author of *A Relationship for a Lifetime,* is a nationally recognized psychiatrist and relationship therapist. He has extensive media experience, having appeared regularly on television shows such as *The Jenny Jones Show* and *Montel* as their "relationship expert." Dr. Johnson's nightly radio show has been based in Chicago for the past decade and is geared toward helping people solve their most difficult relationship, health, and emotional problems. In addition to winning many broadcast awards, this show has consistently been rated the number-one radio talk show in the area.

Since receiving his degree in psychiatry from Northwestern University, Dr. Johnson has maintained a private consultation practice. He lives with his wife, Betsy, and their two dogs in Chicago.

Website: **www.DrKellyJohnson.net**